The Alabama-Coushatta Indians

NUMBER SEVENTY-ONE:
*The Centennial Series
of the Association of Former Students,
Texas A&M University*

The
Alabama-Coushatta
Indians

JONATHAN B. HOOK

Texas A&M University Press
College Station

For Jordan

The paper used in this book meets the minimum requirements
of the American National Standard for Permanence
of Paper for Printed Library Materials, Z39.48-1984.
Binding materials have been chosen for durability.

Library of Congress Cataloging-in-Publication Data

Hook, Jonathan B.
  The Alabama-Coushatta Indians / Jonathan B. Hook.
    p.   cm. — (The centennial series of the Association of Former
Students, Texas A&M University ; no. 71)
    ISBN 0-89096-782-2
    1. Alabama Indians—History. 2. Alabama Indians—Government
relations. 3. Alabama Indians—Ethnic identity. 4. Koasati Indians—
History. 5. Koasati Indians—Government relations. 6. Koasati
Indians—Ethnic identity. I. Title. II. Series.
E99.A4H66   1997
976.4´23504973—dc21   97-25945
                                                              CIP

Contents

Illustrations

Preface

Several years ago I was in Soweto, South Africa, listening to members of the African National Congress articulate their frustration with the Nationalist Party regime and voice their aspirations for a nonracist government. As we sat down at the table in a small, dark room, guards were placed around the block to ensure that there were no surprise visits from the police. It was immediately apparent that living in an urban setting under apartheid had significantly affected their self-perceptions. These young men no longer identified themselves as Zulu or Tswana or Khosa. They were black, a label which included individuals officially designated by the government as "African," "coloured," and "Asian Indian." Personal identity was clearly being influenced by external political and cultural forces.

Especially interested in indigenous responses to European imperialism and colonialism, upon my return to the United States I began an evaluation of the twentieth-century resistance press in southern Africa. My research led me to relocate to Houston, where, because of my Cherokee heritage and tribal membership, I became increasingly active in the American Indian community. Ninety miles northeast of Houston is the Alabama-Coushatta Indian Reservation. There I danced at powwows, worshiped in the Indian Presbyterian Church, chaperoned youth trips, and became involved with a lawsuit intended to ensure that Native American boys could wear their hair long while in school.

The most emotional issues among rural and urban Southeast Texas Native Americans, including repatriation of remains, educational funding, health care, and cultural preservation, in some way address the question of personal identity. Difficulties in determining "who" and "what" are "Indian" continually divide the community. This became for me a compelling issue, and I subsequently changed my research topic to Native American ethnic identity.

In examining American Indian historiography, I was impressed with the stylistic approach of several historians. At a conference on Indian leadership in Chicago sponsored by the D'Arcy McNickle Center of the Newberry Library, R. David Edmunds was a co-participant. He urged us to utilize biographies and solid research in the creation of composite historical scenarios, to set the environmental stage and bring historical characters to life. I found this method helpful in communicating the joy or pathos of a specific historical incident. Calvin Martin, in "The Metaphysics of Writing Indian-White History," (*The American Indian and the Problem of History* [1987]) asks historians to go a step farther: Enter the mind of the subject and thereby experience some elements of his or her culturally derived mental and emotional world. This is difficult to accomplish. While in southern Africa I realized that although I might feel moral outrage at the abuses of apartheid, I could never know the all-encompassing ramifications of being black in the Republic of South Africa. I do, however, know how it feels to be of American Indian descent in white and Indian communities which express little regard for those caught between two cultures:

The middle-aged man spread his starburst-colored Pendleton blanket on the bench, adjusted his mescal-bead bandolier, and looked up at the circling turkey buzzard. Early June in East Texas could be oppressively hot and humid, but these few cool minutes of twilight were perfect. Sunset was almost instantaneous in the Piney Woods, and floodlights were being turned on to illuminate the grassy arena.

The gourd dancer was proud of his new hawk wing fan. He smiled as he removed it from its cedar box and placed it on the bench next to his rattle. He noticed that the fringe at the bottom of his white leather "leggins" dragged the ground too much, and he decided to trim some of it before the next powwow.

"The first set of gourd dancing will begin in five minutes. Singers please head toward the drum," blared the announcer over the scratchy public address system. The dancer felt good, felt that he was a part of the ebb and flow of Indian community life.

He didn't notice the young, blonde-haired couple in blue jeans moving toward the folding lawn chairs immediately behind his bench. They fidgeted somewhat nervously in the new environment, unsure of what to do with the packages just purchased at the vendors' stalls encircling the periphery of the arena. It seemed that all of the craftwork they had bought, dreamcatcher, mandela, flute, and earrings, were decorated with fragile feathers which could easily be misshapen through improper handling. They carefully slid the items under the chairs for protection.

The slim, attractive woman fingered a crystal pendant hanging from a short silver chain around her neck. Only recently had she learned that a powwow was a Native American celebratory dance and not only a slang verb for conversation. She had seen this one advertised in the Houston newspaper and had insisted that they come. Indians and Indian art held a great fascination for her, and she loved novels and movies with Indian settings and motifs. She was especially curious about Indian spirituality and subscribed to several "New Age" popular magazines. Her astrologer assured her that she had been an Indian in a previous incarnation, and there was some mention in her family history of an Indian princess (no one knew which tribe, but probably Cherokee or Sioux).

Still unmindful of the couple, the dancer finished adjusting his intricately embroidered sash. He sat down on the bench and glanced over at the "head" gourd dancer, who was still sorting his "give-a-way" items. Seated at the drum in the center of the arena, the "head" singer finished his second cup of coffee and was ready to begin. Turning his head to smile at a friend sitting behind him, the dancer heard the last words of the woman's remark: ". . . really sad. I thought the dancers were going to be real Indians. Half of these guys are white." The words ripped at his heart. A brief wave of nausea swept over him as he repressed an angry retort. Why couldn't people let him be who he was, an integral part of the Indian community with both Indian and white ancestors. Why was everyone obsessed with skin color? Every time he thought he had come to grips with his own identity, something happened to reopen the wound.

As shown in this composite drawn from my personal experience and multiple interviews with mixed-blood powwow participants, questions of personal identity reach into every niche of the Native American experience, in all geographic and cultural regions. One typical situation is that an individual's ancestors denied their own Indian heritage. Usually employed as a survival tactic in racist white society, it frequently made, and makes, identification with the Indian community difficult for progeny, as Rose Castillo's story, drawn from a personal interview, illustrates:

Rose, the thirty-year-old woman with long black hair and dark skin, sat with her five- and eleven-year-old daughters at the table, waiting for lunch. The white frame Presbyterian Church annex building on the Alabama-Coushatta Reservation in the East Texas Piney Woods was busy with preparations for the monthly "pot-luck" dinner. Fry-bread, chicken-and-dumplings, corn-on-the-cob, sofkee, and yukchee were being uncovered and displayed by dignified, elderly church women. Chief Clayton Sylestine, "Smiley," sat down across from Rose and leaned his cane against the table. "I'm glad you're visiting with us today. If you don't mind telling, what is your heritage?" She paused for a moment, then explained that she had Spanish, French, and Native American blood. Two of her grandparents were Indian, but they were both deceased, and no one in her family ever discussed that side of their ethnicity. She was told that they were from two tribes in Mexico, the Zacatecas and the Huatecas. She wished she knew more, but she didn't. Chief Sylestine said that he understood, and that her situation was not uncommon.

Rose has lived in Houston her entire life. The product of an alcoholic and abusive environment, she struggled to determine her own identity. Raised speaking English and Spanish, she was told she was white and was encouraged to eschew many of her Mexican traditions. The Indian identity of her grandparents was rarely discussed. Subsequent to a failed marriage and another disastrous relationship, she married a Creek-Cherokee-white mixed-blood man who offered her some stability. They began attending the new Native American Methodist Church in Houston and local powwows. Rose indicates that the first time she heard the drum it "spoke to her, called to her." Even though her husband subsequently committed suicide (she thinks partly because of painful insecurities regarding his own identity), he introduced her to the community in which she now finds meaning. Rose works with traditional crafts such as beading, and she and her daughters dance at powwows. She introduces herself as part of the Native American community, rather than as white or Hispanic, though always clarifying that she is of mixed ethnic heritage.

Is Rose Indian? She has no idea of her exact "blood quantum," although it is greater than one-half. She speaks no Indian language and knows none of the customs of her tribe. As an adult, Rose changed her primary ethnic affiliation from white and Hispanic to Native American. She "looks Indian," yet because she is descended from tribes in Mexico, Rose will never be able to produce documentation providing official recognition of Indian heritage in the United States.

The issue of ethnic identity affects people of every language, color, and cultural community. From Dachau to Belfast, Wounded Knee to Lagos, and Jerusalem to Sarajevo, survival frequently depends on perceptions of identity. So it is with Native Americans. Indian identity has ramifications in every area of life, including access to physical, intellectual, and spiritual resources. Life itself often hangs on a thread as tenuous as the style of clothing one wears. Grant Foreman, in his work *Sequoyah* (University of Oklahoma Press [1959]), relates a story in which Sequoyah, the inventor of the Cherokee syllabary, set out in 1842 to find a group of Cherokees rumored to be in Mexico. He became ill and sent the rest of his party to secure some horses so that he could ride. When they arrived in San Antonio, the Cherokees were informed by white soldiers that they would have been fired upon as they approached had it not been for their turbans. It was generally believed that Indians wore no headgear.

Several days later the party encountered Comanches who started to attack the Cherokees, then stopped. "The Comanches then said, that when they first saw us they supposed us to be Texans by having on caps, but when they got nearer and saw feathers in them, they took us to be Shawnees or Delawares, and had it not been for the feathers in our caps, they would have fired upon us." One component of our composite identity is how other ethnic communities perceive us. The Cherokees were not attacked because they were believed to be white by the whites because of their headgear, and they were thought to be Indian by the

Comanches for the same reason. How one is perceived by others is often essential to survival, which is why so many people of Indian ancestry who were light-skinned chose to "pass" as white.

The other factor in determining our identity is how we perceive ourselves, and this self-perception is frequently in a state of transition. I interviewed Zetha Battise, a full-blooded Native American and member of the Alabama-Coushatta tribe:

As Zetha spoke, I looked around the living room of the small frame house where she was born, delivered by her father. Robert Fulton Battise was chief of the Alabama-Coushatta for almost all of her life, and love for her parents is evident in her vibrant and respectful anecdotes about them.

Zetha returned to this, her home, at every opportunity during her career as an elementary school music teacher in New Mexico. Taking early retirement to come home and care for her father, she assumed the role of tribal servant as well, serving on the Tribal Council, the Texas State Textbook Committee, and in any other capacity where she is needed. Several books about the tribe lay stacked on the desk behind an upholstered rocking chair near the doorway to her Aunt Esther's bedroom, but the real history is on the walls.

Photos, gifts, and memorabilia sing of a chief's life dedicated to service and to people. Through the window I see three white-tailed deer, a doe and two fawns, grazing in the late morning shadows at the edge of the yard. They lift their heads briefly as one of the house cats slinks by, chasing an unsuspecting field mouse. The hawk circling overhead also has his eye on supper, but what it is I can't determine. Tall East Texas pines encircle the small clearing of short grass and are reclaiming the western section, formerly used as a garden. In the gathering shadows I can almost hear the words of Chief "Kina" as he speaks with the young boys camped down by Big Sandy Creek, which runs a few hundred yards from the house. Then again, maybe it's just the wind.

Zetha is at home on the reservation. This cultural setting, however, her ancestors from a century earlier would not recognize. Zetha wears "white" clothes purchased from urban department stores, speaks English much of the time, was educated in a university, and worships God by a name other than Abba Mikko in the Presbyterian Church, rather than around a fire. During the past century her people have given up virtually all of their cultural representations, and now, sometimes, she wonders if that was really necessary.

Our self-perception is frequently affected by outside forces such as missionaries and governments, which cause us to alter our personal identity. During the last two decades of the nineteenth century the Alabama-Coushattas converted to Christianity en masse. They surrendered religious festivals and other cultural expressions with millennia-old roots. By 1930 little overt evidence of the old ways remained. Alabama-Coushatta identity, both communal and personal, was dramatically altered through the exertion of external forces and internal responses. Uprooting such deeply entrenched ideology was possible because it was represented as a means of survival in a dominant white society.

Analyzing and depicting this Alabama-Coushatta transition in cultural identity is difficult because of the dearth of written sources. No professional historian has studied or written in depth about the tribe, and magazine and journal articles from early in this century were not scholarly and contained much incorrect information. One important recent source is the work of Howard Martin, who grew up near the reservation and developed a lifelong relationship with the Alabama-Coushattas. He collected and compiled many of their folktales into several published volumes, offered testimony to the Indian Claims Commission on their behalf, and published some well-documented historical research in regional journals. Much respected by the tribe, Martin was designated as the official Alabama-Coushatta tribal historian. This avocational historian and ethnographer was a prolific writer, and his work is invaluable in depicting the history of these Native Americans.

My sources for this project have primarily been the Alabama-Coushatta people themselves. It is their narrative, and they are ultimately the only ones who can adequately depict the movement in their history. I especially wish to thank Zetha and Esther Battise, and Jack and Lawrine Low Battise, for their love and support. Also, I am grateful for the many hours of patience and interesting information given by Dedie Williams and Delores Poncho. Delores is a Navajo (or as they prefer to be called, Dine') who lives on the reservation and is now an adopted Alabama-Coushatta tribal member. Other tribal members whose assistance was invaluable include Chief Clayton Sylestine, Jo Ann Battise, Armando Rodriguez, Dorcas Bullock, Eula Battise, Roland Poncho, Mark Sylestine, Jimmy Johnson, Laurine H. Battise, Deni Sylestine, Frances Battise, Joe and Diane John, and Rochellda Sylestine. Also extremely helpful were former Reservation Superintendent and Texas Indian Commissioner Walter Broemer, and his wife, Frances.

Three organizations that provided much information were the Sam Houston Regional Research Library, the *Polk County Enterprise* newspaper, and the Cook Indian School Library in Tempe, Arizona. Fred Hoxie, former director of the D'Arcy McNickle Center for the History of the American Indian in Chicago, provided tremendous encouragement in the pursuit of this project, as did C. Blue Clark, (Creek) historian and administrator at Oklahoma City University, and University of Kansas sociologist Joane Nagel.

This work would have been impossible without the support of my parents, my wife, Rose, and my children, Jordan, Michelle, and Stephanie, who have endured physical and emotional stress and privation while I struggled with this project. Joe Pryzant provided much moral and economic assistance, for which I am very grateful.

I learned long ago to begin any presentation regarding American Indians with a disclaimer. Native Americans are independent thinkers and articulate spokespeople, and each can communicate for himself or herself. I presume to speak for no tribe or individual other than myself. All opinions expressed in this project are my own, and any mistake in factual representations and interpretation is my responsibility, not that of my sources. Many terms have been used, and are used, to depict the indigenous peoples of this hemisphere. In this paper Native American, American Indian, and Indian are used interchangeably. According to Jack Battise, Alabama-Coushatta elder, the name "Indian" is not a misnomer, but rather is Columbus's complimentary description of the people he encountered as being "*en Dios,*" or People of God. I use the term "Indian" in honor of this interpretation.

As we come to understand the forces which have shaped our cultural and individual identity, we become better equipped to celebrate and lament our past and to prepare for our children's future.

The Alabama-Coushatta Indians

CHAPTER I

Ethnicity
and the American Indian

*. . . I felt, at times, like one who looks into a mirror
and sees a blur over part of his own face. No matter
how he shifts, changes the light, cleans the glass, that area
which cannot be clearly seen remains. And its very
uncertainty becomes more important than that which
is clear and defined in his vision.*

—*Joseph Bruchac,*
Abenaki Metis Writer

The dilemma of cultural identity is arguably the most critical issue in the American Indian world.[1] Intensely emotional and personal, it affects subjects as diverse as self-esteem and distribution of federal resources. The two essential components of the question are deciding who is an Indian (identity) and determining what it means to be Indian (cultural expressions). The present ambiguous status of Indian identity is not an anomaly. It is the logical result of historical forces interacting with the dynamic human creation labeled "culture." Culture is an ongoing process of corporate human expression, comprising individuals who share similar ethnic identities. Ethnic identities are shaped through self-perceptions and by community ascription.

Because culture is a dynamic process, these identities, both corporate and individual, are in a constant state of transition. It is difficult to define the boundaries of an ethnic population because ethnicity is essentially a process of managing relationships across fluid, socially constructed boundaries.[2]

Indian organizations and communities continually struggle over the question of inclusion and over the meaning of their own tribal and Indian identity. What does it mean to be Cherokee or Dine' or Lakota? If language and custom and religion and world view are lost, is the physiological connection enough to make one an Indian?

Whatever the contextually relevant definition for inclusion, the salient points are that Indian identity is fluid and that it is determined by internal and external cultural forces. During the past five hundred years the external forces of greatest impact were disease, European and Euro-American government policy, and missionary proselytizing. The internal cultural responses to these stimuli resulted in dramatic cultural transition and, consequently, in changing individual identity.

Questions of identity and cultural manifestations are inseparable, and frequently incorporate an element of circular reasoning. The cultural practices of those individuals considered to be Indian are used to define Indian characteristics. (i.e., because you are an Indian, you do things in a certain "Indian way.") However, those same Indian cultural manifestations provide the criteria for determining "who" is Indian. (Because you do things in a certain Indian way, you are an Indian.) Both factors, identity and cultural manifestations, are in continual transition, and they are determined by both the Native American and the non-Indian communities. Native American cultural transition and the internal and external forces that propel it are the subject of this study because they provide both illustration and explanation of contemporary Indian identity.

Defining the boundaries for Indian identity is a contentious effort usually concluding with ambiguous results. A general definition of Indian used by the federal government is "a person with some amount of Indian blood who is recognized as an Indian by the person's tribe or community."[3] Tribes and Indian organizations frequently utilize a minimum provable blood quantum as a membership criterion. Disagreement in the various indigenous communities arises because this requirement often excludes those who cannot provide acceptable proof of Indian descent because their ancestors were unable or unwilling to be included on externally derived tribal membership rolls.

A diversity of inclusion definitions is evident throughout Indian country. The most widely used proof of Indian identity is a Certified Degree of Indian Blood (CDIB) card. This document, issued by the federal government, designates the holder to be some specific fraction of Indian blood. Various tribes and Indian organizations may require that members be no less than a stipulated minimum of provable blood quantum. Membership requirements range from those of the Oklahoma Cherokees, who use proof of descent from an ancestor listed on one of the nineteenth- or early twentieth-century tribal census rolls, rather than a specified minimum blood-quantum, to the Alabama-Coushatta Tribe of Texas, which requires that members be full-blooded Indians.[4]

The term "Indian" is a communal designation. Political scientist Ted Robert Gurr defines communal groups as "psychological communities: groups whose core members share a distinctive and enduring collective identity based on cultural traits and lifeways that matter to them and to others with whom they interact."[5]

Analogous to communal identity is ethnic identity. Ethnicity refers to relationships between groups that consider themselves culturally distinct and identifiable and are so regarded by other communities.[6] Similarly, a perceived common origin, common cultural segments, and shared activities denote an ethnic group.[7]

Reservation Indian communities and urban Indian organizations such as the Intertribal Council of Houston, Texas (ITCH), have long agonized over the question of inclusion. Written in 1978, the initial by-laws of ITCH restricted membership to individuals of 1/4 Indian blood or more.[8] Subsequently, their membership guidelines have comprised at various times either three or four levels of membership. ITCH's first level, regular member, includes individuals of 1/4 or more provable Indian blood, *or* membership in a federally recognized tribe. There has been frequent discussion and division since the inception of the organization regarding the word "or." A constant undercurrent of tension regarding the inclusion of tribal members of less than 1/4 quantum as voting members has undermined much creative effort of the organization. Blood quantum questions have disrupted plans ranging from proposed health care to participation in trips funded by outside sources. In November, 1994, one of the officers of the organization suggested that the "regular" membership category be subdivided, allowing those of less than 1/4 Indian blood quantum to vote but not to serve on the board of directors.[9]

The second tier comprises individuals of Indian descent, of any blood quantum, who have no tribal membership and/or supporting documentation. The third category is for non-Indians who are interested in supporting and promoting the goals of the organization. Individuals from these two categories provide most of the volunteer labor to keep the organization functioning.

While ITCH's criteria for full inclusion as "Indian" specify only those of 1/4 or greater blood quantum who are tribe members, the Cherokee Cultural Society of Houston and the American Indian Chamber of Commerce of Texas offer full membership regardless of tribal membership status or blood quantum.[10]

The dilemma of setting inclusion boundaries is not restricted to urban Indian communities. As previously noted, the Cherokee Nation of Oklahoma membership criteria is based on the ability to prove descent from an individual included on the Dawes Roll or an earlier federally recognized census roll. No minimum blood quantum is required. There are many individuals of Cherokee descent, however, whose ancestors did not register on one of the government rolls. These people are permanently excluded from Cherokee tribal membership.[11]

Chad Smith, tribal attorney and recent candidate for Cherokee principal chief, explains that Cherokee tribal membership has traditionally been perceived as inclusion in a political-economic-cultural community. Those who participated in the community were Cherokee.[12] This perspective is evident in early federal attempts at defining tribal inclusion. The 1858 treaty between the United States and the Ponca indicated that those of any blood mixture who desired to reside with the tribe were eligible for full membership. Similarly, the commissioner of Indian Affairs indicated in his 1892 report that Indians were defined as those who lived in tribal relations with other Indians.[13]

The Alabama-Coushatta Tribe of Texas requires that a child be full-blooded Indian for automatic inclusion on the tribal roll at birth. Yet those reservation residents who are less than full blood are perceived to be fully accepted community members.[14] According to Tribal Registrar Yolanda Poncho the tribe is currently issuing membership cards indicating an official degree of Indian blood; the tribe is also revising its constitution to represent more fully the mixed-blood nature of its members.[15]

Ultimately, the definition of "Indian" is contextually determined, and a single set of criteria applicable to all situations is unobtainable. Mixed-blood Indians, both on reservations and in urban Indian communities, continue to be considered suspect by Indians and non-Indians. Terry P. Wilson, a mixed-blood Indian who is a Native American studies professor, explains that individuals claiming to be part of the Indian community but not possessing a stereotypical Indian physical appearance are subjected to suspicion and scrutiny until information about their ancestry, and especially their blood quantum, is offered or discovered.[16]

Perhaps the most visible Indian group struggling for inclusion in the Indian community is the Lumbee tribe of North Carolina. Although they are now accepted in various Native American organizations and by the federal government, their uncertain origins, mixed-blood appearance, and absence of Indian language and custom have long hindered their identification as Indian.[17] Who, then, is Indian?

Equally divisive an issue is the problem of deciding "What is Indian?" Which cultural manifestations, if any, are essential to Indian identity? Which are authentic? How do these cultural representations change over time in response to historical forces?

As a living entity, culture is influenced by both internal and external forces. The two most powerful internal factors are developing physical survival strategies and maintaining continuity with the perceived ethnic past. In every personal and communal historical cultural context, the critical questions are "What must we do to survive," and "What, exactly, defines our ethnic identity, and how can it be maintained?"

The arrival of Columbus in 1492 initiated a period of unprecedented physical and cultural decline for American Indians. Native American groups which could not develop successful survival strategies, including accommodation, frequently disappeared. Although the majority of Cherokees had adopted many white sociopolitical practices, several hundred Cherokees demurred and chose to relocate in 1819–20 to present Texas. In 1839, after a military encounter with the militia of the new Republic of Texas, those remaining alive were forced to emigrate to Indian territory. Their overt attempt to retain traditional culture and practice had failed.[18] Charles Boudreaux claims that his ancestors were among a small number of these Cherokees who remained in Texas. They developed survival strategies rooted in assimilation and adaptation. They spoke English, pursued "white" education, and explained their dark skin claiming "Black Dutch" heritage.[19]

On a communal level, Indian survival necessitated a dramatic disruption of life-ways, although not the complete surrender of cultural practice. While material and political aspects of Indian culture changed, much of Indian cultural life remained intact.[20] In the implementation of survival strategies vis-à-vis the United States, Indian leaders frequently walked a narrow path between self-effacement and dignity. Comanche leader Quanah Parker could play the role of "obsequious subordinate" in relating with white officials, while maintaining considerable pride and self-assurance.[21]

These strategies were, and are, costly when cultural identity is surrendered to ensure physical survival. Chippewa pipe carrier and assistant medicine man Larry P. Aitken suggests that at the individual level, losing one's cultural identity is comparable to being banished from the community. It causes intellectual confusion and emotional grief.[22]

As cultural representations and practices change, so does personal identity. Illustrative of this is the Dine' *Kinaalda* ceremony, a rite signifying a young girl's transition to puberty. Dine' society is matrilineal and matrilocal, and this ceremony remains firmly entrenched. It has, however, changed considerably within recent memory. Anthropologist Charlotte Frisbie lists seventeen changes between the "old way" and "new way." These include alterations in attire, music, and procedures. Perhaps the most significant change she indicates is the acceptance of the consumption of alcohol.[23] Once conducted solemnly and with the expression of taboos, the ceremony is now an occasion for excessive drinking. One informant suggests that heavy drinkers frequently "ruin" the whole observance.[24] Respect, an essential attribute in Native America, is lost, reducing the girl's self-esteem and altering her perception of personal identity.[25] The situation is part of a cultural milieu in which suicide rates reach as high as 17 percent of the teenaged population in some Indian communities.[26]

Just as there are diverse perceptions among urban Indian organizations and tribes regarding Indian identity, those definitions and perceptions of "Indianness" are themselves constantly in transition. Our ethnic identity changes from situational context to context and across time. As groups surrender various cultural expressions such as attire, religious expression, language, and music, they may believe themselves to be less recognizable as that specific cultural entity. The force for survival has outweighed the force to maintain overt cultural representations.[27]

When physical survival is no longer the paramount issue, however, cultural survival may then become the highest priority, and a regenesis of that culture, or an ethnogenesis, takes place. Regenesis denotes the reintroduction of cultural practices formerly observed by the group. Ethnogenesis indicates the intentional introduction of cultural practices that lead to the creation of a new cultural identity. These two phenomena frequently coexist. Regenesis usually includes extensive research into specific tribal practices in order to restore them into tribal life. Ethnogenesis is the implementation of cultural practices that were not a part of a group's cultural heritage. For Native Americans, these may include stereotypical clothing and artifacts expected by tourists and also the adoption of powwow and other pan-Indian expressions of art, music, attire, and religion.

Precursors to ethnogenesis are evident in millenialist movements such as the "ghost dance" of the Plains Indians. The creation and introduction of this religious practice foreshadowed the emergence of the Native American Church and renewed interest in other Indian religious beliefs.[28]

Today, ethnogenesis and regenesis are visible in dances based on older forms of expression, in language classes, in revitalization of craftwork, and in restoration of former and borrowed religious expressions. Anthropologist Margaret Mead noted that in the 1930s oil-rich Oklahoma Indians bought theatrical Indian costumes for poorer members of other tribes to wear at special events.[29] While participants and their activities may be considered authentic by those taking part and by observers, in a very real sense modern

Indian culture is a hybridization, a unique entity deriving from Western European[30] and indigenous cultures. The aforementioned Cherokee, Charles Boudreaux, believes that he no longer needs to hide his Indian ancestry in order to survive. He is active in the Southeast Texas Indian community in both Cherokee and supra-tribal activities.[31]

The process of Indian ethnogenesis is evident throughout the continent. The two prevalent characteristics of indigenous ethno-genesis are the apparent loss of "traditional" tribal cultural prac-tices that are replaced with more assimilated expressions, and the emergence and growth of a supratribal Indian identity.

Sociologist Eugeen Roosens describes this phenomenon among the Hurons, whom he found to have been mixing with Europeans for three centuries, "so that none of the residents of the Huron Village could be identified by an outsider as being phenotypically Indian." Most worked outside the Huron com-munity and "differed only minimally from the culture of the sur-rounding French Canadians." They had lost their Indian language completely, and Roosens "sought in vain for traces of the former religion and of the traditional family system."

Yet the Hurons had assumed leadership of the *Association des Indiens du Quebec*. They fought diligently for native rights and were in the process of intentionally developing a Huron "coun-terculture." Virtually every characteristic of this neoculture was a recent creation or adaptation: "the folklore articles, the hair style, the moccasins, the 'Indian' parade costumes, the canoes, the pot-tery, the language, the music." Roosens characterizes all of these as "attempts to introduce a perceptible difference between the Hurons and the surrounding Canadians in a way that suggests some Indian stereotype."[32] What made them distinctly Huron was (is) the close tie to the land: continuity of residence on the reservation. The community had existed, exists, and would con-tinue to exist. Artifacts could be reinvented and revised: toma-hawks, canoes, and headdresses targeted for sale to tourists consist of manmade materials, and the popular fringed leather jackets share little similarity with former Huron clothing.[33]

While the modern Hurons were virtually indistinguishable culturally and physiologically from the surrounding Europeans, they nevertheless retained their identification with the land and with the community. The conscious creation of a neo-Huron identity in the second half of the twentieth century was engendered by the dialectic synthesis of predominantly French Europeans and Huron Indians. Today that community remains "Huron" while engaging in cultural practices that would have been alien to their immediate ancestors.

A second characteristic of Indian ethnogenesis, apparently antithetical yet coexisting with increased assimilation, is the growth of supratribal consciousness. There was no indigenous term for Native American, or Indian, in pre-Colombian America. Vine Deloria, Jr. (Native American historian and Standing Rock Sioux), suggests that "'Indianness' never existed except in the mind of the [white] beholder."[34] Each ethnic and linguistic group tended to be ethnocentric. *Kiowa* means "the principal people," as does *ani yun wiya*, which the Cherokees call themselves. Distinct cultural boundaries existed between Indian nations, whose languages and lifestyles were much more diverse than those of the multinational European invaders. There simply was no universal concept of "American Indian."

Although there are earlier examples of joint Indian activities,[35] widespread pan-Indian consciousness did not occur until the latter half of the twentieth century. In his book *The Return of the Native: American Indian Political Resurgence* (1988), Stephen Cornell suggests that a distinct Indian identity, evidenced by cooperative political efforts among various Indian organizations, "has become a conscious and important basis of action and thought in its own right."[36]

The prevalence of supratribal consciousness is particularly evident in the urban context. Many urban organizations are intertribal in nature. In Houston, Texas, there are two supratribal social organizations, an Indian Baptist mission, an American Indian Chamber of Commerce, and two Native American student groups. Rural and reservation activities that also indicate a strong supratribal consciousness include powwows, Indian churches, intertribal organizations, Indian Chambers of Commerce, art and craft shows, and joint political and legal actions.

The growth of supratribalism has not, however, hastened assimilation to the point of loss of personal tribal associations. Although there are some individuals who claim to be Native American but have little or no connection to a specific tribe, for the overwhelming majority tribal affiliation enables participation in urban Indian activities and provides legitimacy for supratribal involvement. Ties to tribal communities are strong, and many Indians frequently return to tribal areas to visit or reside for a period of time.[37]

This continued tribal identification for Indians is as relevant for mixed-blood, multigenerational urban dwellers as for reservation residents. Tribal association of some sort is usually the minimum criteria for inclusion in the urban Indian community. For example, in 1993 Northern Arizona University developed and administered a survey of Disabled Native Americans in the Houston area. A group of American Indians from the Houston community was invited to form the committee that subsequently debated the criteria to determine participant inclusion.

Some committee members felt that a CDIB, 1/4 blood quantum, or tribal membership should be required. Others believed that no one who claimed to be of Indian descent should be excluded from the survey. It was finally decided that anyone who claimed descent from a specific tribe, and who could identify that tribe, would be eligible. All that a potential interviewee need do was say "I am Apache," or "Cherokee." Those who indicated Indian ancestry but were unable to identify the tribe were disqualified.[38] Tribal identity is not lost in the process of ethnogenesis or regenesis, it is the necessary antecedent.

Increased coercive assimilation and voluntary adaptation resulted in the loss of specific cultural artifacts such as language, dance, songs, art, attire, and religious belief. Some native groups, like the Hurons, utilize cultural forms that are stereotypical (what the tourists expect), or that derive from pan-Indian identity and participation (powwow dances and regalia). The construction of a new ethnicity with strong supratribal influence while retaining tribal identity is facilitated by various cultural construction processes. Sociologist Joane Nagel identifies four:

> Among the major types are cultural revivals, restorations, revisions, and innovations. *Cultural revivals* occur when lost or forgotten cultural forms or practices are excavated and reintroduced into ongoing cultural activities. *Cultural restorations* occur when

lapsed or occasional cultural forms or practices are renovated and reintegrated into ongoing cultural activities. *Cultural revisions* occur when current elements of culture are changed or adapted and retained as part of ongoing culture. *Cultural innovations* occur when new cultural forms or practices are created and integrated into ongoing or newly established cultural traditions.[39]

Cultural revivals, restorations, and revisions could best be labeled as components of regenesis. On the other hand, cultural innovation is ethnogenesis.

An example of cultural revival is the use of eighteenth- and nineteenth-century written accounts of Cherokee religious beliefs and practices by contemporary Cherokees in their attempt to become more "traditional." This is especially evident among the urban population, who may not have access to oral sources, and who, because of extensive assimilation and a mixed-blood heritage, may feel more comfortable with a Eurocentric learning style.

During the worship service of the short-lived (summer, 1992) Native American Methodist Church of Houston, cedar was frequently burned as part of the ritual, and a feather prayer fan was used.[40] These are examples of cultural restoration of practices long associated with Native American religious activity.

As the powwow movement spread throughout the southwestern United States, one cultural form frequently associated with it was "gourd dancing." Introduced and spread by the "KCAs" (Kiowa-Comanche-Apache), many non-Plains tribes now have gourd dance societies (e.g., Alabama-Coushattas and Cherokees).[41] In this cultural revision many southeastern Indians (descendants of the so-called five "civilized" tribes), especially urban residents, participate more frequently in powwows and gourd dances than in stomp dances, their own traditional ceremony.[42]

A component of the 1994 Indian Days celebration near the Coushatta Reservation in Louisiana was a performance by a gospel singing group.[43] Similarly, gospel singing has long been a component of the Cherokee National Homecoming celebration.[44] This is an example of cultural innovation.

In the popular mythology of the United States's image as a great cultural melting pot, it was generally assumed that cultural distinctions would gradually disappear, and that ethnic-oriented behavior would cease. This did not happen, and the melting pot metaphor was being challenged by the early 1960s.[45] Ethnic behavior persists, as do ethnic distinctions. The current cultural and political climate accepts and often celebrates ethnic diversity, even among whites.[46]

Anthropologist Richard Thompson defines ethnic behavior as those actions that are "at a *minimum*, based on *cultural or physical criteria in a social context in which these criteria are relevant*,"[47] and suggests several models to explain the persistence of ethnic identity.

Two of these, the sociobiological theory and the primordial sentiments theory, he labels as "natural." Three others, "assimilationist," "world system," and "Marxian," he calls social theories. In the "natural" models ethnic identity is inherited, and in the "social" models it is socially constructed.

No one model adequately explains the persistence of Native American ethnic identity. There is a widespread belief that Indian identity requires a blood connection because there are essential genetically transmitted cultural memories.[48] Kiowa author N. Scott Momaday suggests that Indian identity is intricately interconnected with a "spiritual sense so ancient as to be primordial, so pervasive as to be definitive."[49] Much of the ethnogenesis and regenesis evident today is rooted in personal rediscovery of the salience of Indian religious belief. Lakota activist Mary Crow Dog states that modern Indian resurgence "was first of all a spiritual movement and that our ancient religion was at the heart of it."[50] There is no real conflict between the physiological and the cultural facets of ethnicity, because biological and cultural transmission are often simultaneously experienced.[51] For whatever reason, ethnic identity persists in a dynamic form.

The inherently mutable nature of ethnicity combined with external cultural forces makes the issue of identity as emotional and ambiguous as it is pervasive and transitional. Consider the following illustration of a young Indian dancer, a composite drawn from numerous case studies:

He leaned back in the folding lawn chair, away from the large drum at the center of the floor, moved the microphone out of the way, and motioned for the arena director to hand him a cup of coffee. The old gymnasium was filled with powwow spectators and dancers, and a few vendors of feathers, beads, and other regalia components. Reaching back to ensure that his feather bustle with its orange and green streamers hadn't fallen from the back of the chair, he then adjusted his head roach, arm bands, "leggins" and plastic hairpipe breastplate. They had sung several northern-style songs while the women competed, now he needed to mentally prepare for his fancy-dance contest.

While the young Alabama Indian dancer straightened his regalia, he thought briefly about his great-great grandfather. He doubted that his ancestor would even recognize him. Instead of Alabama buckskins, he was wearing Lakota-inspired ceremonial clothing held together in some places with safety-pins and duct tape. English had replaced Albamu, of which he knew only a few words. He listened to rock music instead of tribal songs, and his powwow dances came from Plains Indian traditions rather than from the southeastern "stomp". A Christian, at least in name, he practiced none of the old purification rites. His was a matrilineal tribe, and since his father was Indian but his mother was not, he was not eligible for clan membership. He had never worked in a corn field, nor had he ever killed a deer. Sometimes he wondered exactly what being Alabama Indian meant.[52]

The Alabama-Coushatta Indians of East Texas are an appropriate subject for a study of the dynamic nature of culture because they are a microcosm for the experiences of most American Indian nations. Their history may be divided into four post-contact cultural periods:

(1) initial contact and migration,
(2) early reservation and missionary presence,
(3) Indian New Deal, World War Two, and federal Termination, and
(4) regenesis/ethnogenesis.

In each of these periods external forces exerted sufficient pressure to exact cultural change. The most frequently attacked and consistently undermined Alabama-Coushatta cultural value was that of community.

Following initially violent confrontations with Europeans, the Alabamas and Coushattas developed cordial relations with one or more of the European powers. Subsequently induced to migrate west, they were placed on a reservation in present Texas. There, the tribe converted to Christianity through the long-term efforts of missionaries. Later, acting upon Indian Commissioner John Collier's Indian New Deal model, they developed a Tribal Council and incorporated. In the 1950s their formal trust relationship with the federal government was dissolved, although three decades later they were again federally recognized. Today tourism and mineral exploitation constitute a large percentage of tribal economic activity. The elder generation speaks a traditional language, but the youth speak primarily English.

The tribes retained their traditional beliefs and practices relatively intact until the last two decades of the nineteenth century. They could do so because they were physically isolated from non-Indian influences and also because they heeded Sam Houston's admonition to never let a white man reside with them. Missionary efforts beginning in the 1880s proved to be the greatest challenge to Alabama-Coushatta cultural continuity.

During the first twenty years of missionary activity the number of Christians in the community grew from zero to "all-save-one." The entire tribe had converted. Although the missionaries were not racist (they believed that the Indians could become as completely "civilized" as the whites), they were extremely ethnocentric and attempted to eradicate virtually all cultural expression. The Indians were told to relinquish their faith in traditional healing, give up Indian sports, wear European-style clothing, speak English, and forego all traditional religious practices (which, at least superficially, they did). The most dangerous Indian ideology to Euro-American cultural hegemony was the ascendant role of community. Missionaries, and subsequently the government, sought to replace this value with emphasis on the individual, with dramatic implications for personal identity.

In the late 1950s the reservation superintendent advocated a switch from agriculture to tourism as the primary economic activity. This transition brought many non-Indians onto the reservation, both as tourists and as laborers. The process of ethnogenesis introduced pan-Indian and supratribal practices such as the exhibition of Plains Indian "powwow"-type dances for tourists. This coincided with the nationwide growth of the powwow movement as inter-Indian intercourse expanded.

Today many reservation youth know numerous powwow songs

and dances, but they have retained few Alabama-Coushatta songs or dances. English has become the *lingua franca* of Indian youth; very few still speak Albamu. The newly emerged identity takes pride in being Indian, but it is a persona that often retains few remnants of specific Indian culture.

American Indian cultures comprise communal and individual ethnic identities that are shaped by one's personal perceptions, by non-Indian community perceptions, and by Native American community perceptions. These identities and their composite culture are dynamic, living entities struggling for both physical and cultural survival. Cultural transition occurs when external forces cause survival strategies to be enacted. These changes may be experienced in any, and in virtually all, areas of lived experience. In the case of the Alabamas and Coushattas, this cultural movement and its causes may be traced over a period of three hundred years. Change agents (external forces), particularly Christian missionaries and government agents, caused cultural transition in areas including religious belief and practice, attire, language, location, and medical practices. Over time, these cultural transformations dramatically altered the Alabama-Coushatta perception of Indian identity.

The object of this study is to depict the dynamic nature of culture. The subject is the Alabama-Coushatta Indian community of southeast Texas. They have responded to external forces through enacting communal and personal survival strategies. These strategies include contemporary tribal regenesis and ethnogenesis. Individual identity derives from identification with a specific cultural entity. The dynamic nature of culture causes personal identity to be in a constant state of transition. The case study of the Alabama-Coushatta Indians of East Texas provides a vivid example of this phenomenon.

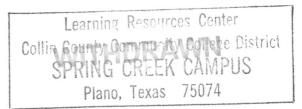

CHAPTER 2

Early Contact
to Reservation Establishment
The Alabama-Coushatta Experience

In the beginning the world was covered with darkness.
There was no sun, no day. The perpetual night had
no moon or stars. There were, however, all manner
of beasts and birds. Among the beasts were many hideous,
nameless monsters. . . Mankind could not prosper under
such conditions, for the beasts and serpents destroyed
all human offspring.

—*Geronimo,*
Apache Leader

From their first encounter with Europeans, Alabama-Coushatta lives were altered. During the early contact and migration periods these external forces were not sufficient to completely displace native culture and replace it with that of the Europeans. The transition in cultural identity, however, had begun.

A chronological organizational approach to the depiction of Alabama-Coushatta cultural change is essentially non-Indian in concept, as is the categorization of life-ways for analytical purposes. Native American perception of time was, and for some still is, cyclical rather than linear, and the Indian world view is holistic rather than compartmentalized. The circle is extremely significant in Native American thinking and culture. Black Elk, a Lakota medicine man, explains its universal cultural relevance to Indians:

"You have noticed that everything an Indian does is in a circle, and that is because the Power of the World always works in circles, and everything tries to be round. . . . Everything the Power of the World does is done in a circle. The sky is round, and I have heard that the earth is round like a ball, and so are all the stars. . . . The life of a man is a circle from childhood to childhood, and so it is in everything where power moves."[1]

But, as another Lakota medicine man, John Lame Deer, explains, western society is rooted in a dramatically different world view:

> The white man's symbol is the square. Square is his house, his office buildings with walls that separate people from one another. Square is the door which keeps strangers out, the dollar bill, the jail. Square are the white man's gadgets—boxes, boxes, boxes and more boxes—TV sets, radios, washing machines, computers, cars. These all have corners and sharp edges—points in time, white man's time, with appointments, time clocks and rush hours—that's what the corners mean to me. You become a prisoner inside all these boxes.[2]

Historians utilizing a Western European analytical paradigm possess a different ideology than do most American Indians.[3] This makes it difficult to write an Indian history that incorporates a Native American world view. It is also difficult to present Native American history from an Indian perspective that is also acceptable and intelligible to the Euro-american community. These two problems point to the cultural disparity between Indian and white culture. Most written descriptions of the Alabama-Coushattas were by non-Indian observers whose observations of native culture were ethnocentric. These documents do, however, provide sufficient information to allow comparisons with subsequent Alabama-Coushatta cultural expressions.

Pre-contact Alabama and Coushatta history is essentially unknown, even to tribal members.[4] According to one of their traditions, Abba Mikko created the people from clay, and they lived in a deep underground cave for a long time. Then they moved upward toward the cave entrance. Standing at the entrance was a large tree or root, and as the people emerged from the cave they divided, some going to the right of the tree and some to the left.

This is how one people became two nations, the Alabamas and the Coushattas. Soon, however, they heard an owl (the harbinger of death) screech, and many hurried back to the safety of the cave and remained there. That is why there are so few Alabamas and Coushattas today.[5]

As inheritors of the Mississippian mound-building legacy and of Cahokia's Southeastern ceremonial complex, the Muskogean-speaking Alabama and Coushatta nations exerted considerable regional influence in what subsequently became the states of Alabama and Mississippi. Ethnographer John R. Swanton stated that "next to the Muskogee themselves the most conspicuous Upper Creek tribe were the Alabama, or Albamo."[6]

The first European-derived external force for cultural change among the Alabamas and Coushattas was probably the diseases introduced into the hemisphere during the first three decades of the sixteenth century. The Spaniards brought pathogens against which Native Americans had little or no immunity. These outran their European hosts, causing extensive decimation of native communities.[7] Demographer Henry Dobyns estimates that a sixteenth-century North American Indian population of 18 million was reduced to between 250,000 and 300,000 by the nineteenth century,[8] while historian Russell Thornton suggests a 1492 western hemisphere population of over 72 million, with a more conservative number of 7 million in North America. He estimates that this latter population was reduced to between 125,000 and 150,000 by 1900.[9]

These diseases began the transition of Indian culture by European change agents by altering the composition of the town populations, by restructuring political and social associations, and by compromising the perceived efficacy of traditional religio-medical practices. Disease decimated towns, depriving them of clan, political, military, and religious leaders. Remnants of communities fled to other groups and attempted to form new alliances. Traditional medical providers, who frequently died themselves, could offer no hope for the afflicted. Culture was dramatically altered before the first European footstep was heard in the town square.

This turmoil opened the door to European ideological influence. In 1535 or 1536 Cabeza de Vaca and other shipwreck survivors enjoyed great success as shamans and healers among Texas Indians because they were perceived to be more powerful than the native medicine men and women.[10] This is an early example of Europeans working as cultural change agents among Native Americans. The diseases that de Vaca observed possibly spread north and east. These could have been the source of the epidemics that decimated the Creeks from 1536–39, predating face-to-face contact by as much as a decade.[11] Smallpox epidemics began in the northern nations in 1520–24 and were rapidly followed by measles, influenza, and typhus.[12] Europeans had some experience in dealing with epidemics, and James Adair, who lived with the southeastern Indians during the mid-eighteenth century, stated that the European traders among the Creeks "have taught them to prevent the last contagion from spreading among their towns, by cutting off all communication with those who are infected, till the danger is over."[13]

There is no written material indicating the population of precontact, pre-epidemic Alabama and Coushatta communities. According to Alabama-Coushatta tribal elder Jack Battise, oral tradition indicates that both entities were much larger before being reduced, first by disease, and later through attrition during the migration period.[14] Although there are no records indicating early Alabama-Coushatta population, Spanish references to various Alabama and Coushatta towns indicate significant regional numbers.

Hernando de Soto was the first known European to encounter the Alabama and Coushatta nations, and thus he was the first to directly influence their culture. In 1540 he and his entourage of over one thousand heavily armed soldiers, servants, and Indian porters (frequently abducted from towns through which he passed) found some Coushatta (cited by various European chroniclers as Coste, Acoste, Costehe, Coosada, Conshata, Couchati, Conchaty, Koasati, and Coushatta) living on an island in the Tennessee River. The chief of the Coushatta town welcomed the Spaniards in peace and invited them to sleep in an outlying village.

This response to the strangers is indicative of a cultural value exhibited by the Alabamas for a half-millennium. Maintaining peace, frequently at the expense of self-effacement, is evident throughout the long period of interaction with non-Indians.

However, peaceful intentions did not preclude the use of physical force when it was deemed necessary.

While in the town, the European guests stole some corn, an event that almost precipitated conflict with the townspeople. De Soto was able to prevent violence by appearing to chastise the thieves.[15] Thus began direct interaction between the two cultures.

In 1541 De Soto engaged in a battle with some Alabamas at their fortified town somewhere between the Yazoo and Tombigbee rivers in present Mississippi. A contemporary observer, Biedma, stated that three hundred warriors engaged in the action in order to test the strength of the Spaniards and that many of the Indians were killed.[16] Another early source, the Knight of Elvas, described the Indians as having "their bodies, legs, and arms painted and ochered, red, black, white, yellow, and vermillion in stripes, so that they appeared to have on stockings and doublet." They also wore feathers and some had horns on their heads.[17] In this initial contact period the greatest direct cultural influence was the introduction of new military technology, including weapons, armor, and transportation. This was possibly the Indians' first exposure to the European concept of war, one which inflicted great numbers of casualties on combatants and non-combatants alike.

No extant references exist for these tribes from 1541 until the early eighteenth century, and by that time the two Indian nations, or portions thereof, had relocated farther south to the upper section of the Alabama River.[18] During the late seventeenth century the English established settlements along the Atlantic coast. From these villages traders plied their wares of cloth, ammunition, guns, and rum throughout Creek territory. It is likely that the Alabamas and Coushattas first encountered the English at this time.[19] The French arrived at Mobile Bay in 1702 and built Fort St. Louis de la Mobile. In 1703 the Alabamas allied with the English and skirmished with the French.[20] The use of European trade goods suggests that cultural transition was in progress, especially in the areas of attire and weaponry. A general anti-English sentiment subsequent to the 1714–15 Yamasee War[21] was exploited by the French, and that year they built Fort Alabama, or Fort Toulouse (near present-day Montgomery, Alabama) on the east bank of the Coosa River.[22]

Representatives of the group that eventually became the greatest cultural change agent among the Alabama-Coushattas, Christian missionaries, arrived during this period. The French contingent at Fort Toulouse included several priests, but squabbling between military and religious personnel may have prevented any real proselytizing efforts during this first contact with the Christian religion.[23] There is no evidence of conversions among the Alabamas and Coushattas, and sustained missionary effort with these two tribes did not occur for another 150 years. Fort Toulouse remained under French control until the Treaty of Paris was signed in 1763, placing the territory under English authority.

Subsequent Protestant missionary and government efforts during the nineteenth and twentieth centuries significantly altered Alabama-Coushatta society. In order to analyze the cultural transition effected by these and other non-Indian change agents, it is necessary to depict Alabama-Coushatta cultural life during the early contact period. This will provide an ethnic illustration with which later cultural expressions may be compared and contrasted.

The Alabamas and Coushattas were part of the Creek Confederacy, a loose trade and sometimes military organization of autonomous towns. In the early 1770s botanist William Bartram estimated that in the fifty-five Creek towns there were eleven thousand inhabitants.[24]

Creek towns contained a public square surrounded by four rectangular buildings (not every Indian structure was round). These buildings were partitioned into three compartments (called "cabins"). The center cabin on the east side was reserved for the "beloved men" of the town and was called the "beloved seat." Renowned soldiers sat in the cabins on the south side, and the "second men" (the chiefs' advisors) were in the compartments on the north side. The building to the west was used to store lumber and miscellaneous military materials. Some towns had covered squares with cane roofs.

A representative of the United States Army, Maj. Caleb Swan, visited Creek towns in the early nineteenth century and found a consistent layout. At the southwest corner of the square was the chunkey, or ball-play, yard, and at the northwest corner sat the sweat, or round, house. The round house was a circular-based pyramid about twenty-five feet high, inside which men conversed and danced for hours.[25] At the center of the floor of this council house a "mystical" fire was tended, political affairs were conducted, and the pipe was smoked.[26]

Botanist William Bartram said that women were not allowed inside the round house, but eighteenth-century French traveler Jean-Bernard Bossu related one instance where "the wife of a great chief used to attend these assemblies as a warrior because of her quick and penetrating mind. Sometimes it was her opinion that prevailed in treaty making."[27] The subversion of the political power of native women was one of the first cultural changes effected by contact with Europeans, who were unwilling to acknowledge their structural role.[28]

Chunkey was a game in which small, polished-stone disks were rolled along the ground. Poles were thrown at them and points scored. In the center of the chunkey yard was a pole, approximately thirty feet tall, used for archery contests. Stickball (*tele*), the forerunner of modern lacrosse, was also played on the field, with inter-town rivalries sometimes becoming quite heated.[29] Also situated in the chunkey yard were shorter poles to which captives were bound before execution or enslavement. Dances were held in the chunkey yard during warm months.[30]

William Bartram described Alabama houses as "neat commodious buildings, a wooden frame with plaistered walls, and roofed with Cypress bark or shingles."[31] Four rectangular buildings surrounding a courtyard comprised the family dwelling. This layout remained consistent in Alabama-Coushatta towns until the twentieth century, and it reinforced common religious, political, athletic, and military values. These activities emphasized and strengthened communal life. Team achievement was perceived to be greater than individual victory. Athletes were valued for their athletic prowess, but always in the greater context of the community.

Alabama and Coushatta towns were divided into "red" and "white" designations. White towns were responsible for maintaining peace and providing refuge, and red towns conducted military campaigns. The Alabama thought of themselves as essentially peace loving and according to Jean-Bernard Bossu, called their home the "white land, or the land of peace."[32]

The *mikko* was the town leader. He was selected on the basis of oratorical skills and general popularity. A "second chief," or "town chief," was usually chosen to assist the mikko. A group of "second men" provided advice, and a military commander was appointed by the mikko. Each mikko was an autonomous leader; because of this, an early French attempt to consolidate Alabama power under a single individual, designated the Alabama "emperor," failed completely.[33] Once again, the cultural value of community precluded the elevation of one person to a significantly higher status.

The law of retaliation was vigorously enforced. This applied to all injuries, from the most heinous crime to the least minor accident. Trader James Adair related an incident illustrating this concept. While a young boy was shooting birds in a densely grown cornfield, he inadvertently injured another youth. The "wound was returned in as equal a manner as could be expected." This fulfilled the law and "all was straight," then "they sported together as before."[34]

All crimes except murder (which was punished with death), however, were forgiven at the time of the green corn festival, and some towns were designated as places of sanctuary.[35] According to James Adair, these provided "a sure asylum to protect a man-slayer, or the unfortunate captive, if they can once enter into it."[36]

Alabama and Coushatta economic pursuits included gathering, hunting, agriculture, fishing, and trading. A meal might include mush made of corn, venison, corn bread, turkey, bread fried in oil, chestnuts, turtle or hen eggs, and pumpkins.[37] Men did the hunting, but their families went along on extended hunting trips. The game most sought was deer (for its meat), bear (for its oil), and turkey. Deer were called or rattled close enough for a shot, and deer decoys were also utilized. Coushatta bows were straight, with no curvature at the tips.[38] Cane-shafted arrows were tipped with fire-hardened points, gar scales, or bone.[39] Fish were gigged with sharpened cane spears tied to bark cords, or with bows and arrows. The meat and fish were smoked and distributed among friends and the elderly.[40] This illustrates the strength of the communal ethic, which demanded that resources be shared.

Young men and women were sexually active before marriage. In this matri-clan society, identification of paternity was not critical. White visitors were offered the company of their host's daughters, the latter being exhorted by the chief to have intercourse with their European guests so that mixed-blood children would be born.[41] After marriage men and women were expected to be faithful, although a man was permitted to have more than one wife, and wives could be loaned to special friends.[42] This social pattern reinforced interdependence rather than individual male possession of a spouse.

Marriage was not initiated with an extensive religious or civil ceremony but was marked by mutual agreement of the involved parties, a gift exchange, and a large meal to which all townspeople were invited.[43] Adultery was punished with varying degrees of severity. Jean-Bernard Bossu described one incident in which the guilty pair was beaten and the woman's hair shorn.[44] James Adair stated that according to some middle-aged Creeks infidelity was previously punished by death. The great number of male transgressors, however, necessitated a reduction in the penalty to preclude a significant reduction in their military force. After a woman was proven to have committed adultery, "the enraged husband accompanied by some of his relations, surprises and beats her most barbarously, and then cuts off her hair and nose, or one of her lips."[45]

Burial rites were extensive. The deceased was buried in a sitting position,[46] along with important personal items. Other gifts or personal possessions were placed on top of the grave. Alabamas and Coushattas believed that a person had two souls. One would go immediately to the afterlife location upon death. The other would remain by the body for four days and could possibly become a ghost. For four evenings a male relation would fire four shots toward the west, the direction of the journey after death. The first day the spirit awoke, the second it stood, the third it assembled its possessions, and on the fourth it departed.

Ritual cleansing of surviving family and friends was performed through medicine and vomiting, and the period of mourning could last from one to four years.[47] A widow was required to remain single and chaste for four years. However, if after a year she could convince her husband's eldest brother to have sexual intercourse with her, she was freed from further mourning.[48]

The clan moiety was an egalitarian matri-clan system, with each kinship group consisting of many families. Alabama and Coushatta clans were completely exogamous: Marriage within the clan was absolutely taboo. Clan elders frequently formed a community council to advise the mikko, whose power rested solely in his oratorical power to persuade. Although the decision-making tribal council was composed exclusively of men, women played a major role in the political process through the influence of the clans.[49]

Women possessed the houses and permanently resided in them. According to ethnographer John Swanton, the "typical Creek home would . . . consist of a man and a woman, their children, one or more sons-in-law, some grandchildren, some aged or dependent individuals of the same clan group, and perhaps an orphan or two or one or more individuals taken in war." The latter were "rapidly assimilated with the tribe. . . ."[50]

James Adair stated that Indians believed themselves "a peculiar and beloved people" of God, and they "are exceedingly intoxicated with religious pride."[51] The "Master of Life," (also called the Master of Breath) the creator and life-giver, may have been associated with the sun, or the "Power behind the Sun," and his worship played a role in virtually every facet of life. Other lesser supernatural beings were also recognized.[52]

All of the central rites of Creek religious practice involved purification. Sweats, bathing, and ingestion of the black drink served to cleanse from personal pollution. This emphasis may have indicated both a societal sense of unworthiness and culpability and may reveal a cosmology that was essentially forgiving.[53]

The "busk" (from the Creek boshita, "fast"), or green corn dance, was the greatest corporate expression of purification. Held annually, it included cleansing through ingestion and regurgitation of the "black drink" (which Jean-Bernard Bossu and Caleb Swan identify as cassina, *Ilex vomitoria*, or yaupon holly),[54] general amnesty (except for murder),[55] and rekindling of the sacred fire.[56]

The busk fulfilled many communal needs. Focusing on the new crop of corn, it revered fertility and continued well-being. It encouraged social unity and health, promoted peace with other Confederacy towns, and honored the clans and elders. An opportunity for celebration, visiting, and feasting, it brought the Master of Breath into the community, into the fire. Old transgressions were expiated, and a new period of purity and moral living was ushered in. The early busks also included the initiation of young men into a military class and the symbolic killing of enemies.[57] It was the personal and communal religious climax of the year.[58]

Many of these cultural expressions began to change in the latter seventeenth century as a period of westward migration began. At the conclusion of the Seven Years' War in 1763, France ceded southern Alabama to England and Louisiana to Spain. George III's Proclamation of 1763 established the Appalachian Mountains as a dividing line between Indian territory and land authorized for British settler occupation. The proclamation was largely ignored by English colonists, who soon flooded the region.

Honoring their fifty-year relationship and alliance with the French, the Alabamas and Coushattas began a westward movement in order to avoid British sovereignty.[59] The restructuring of European political influence caused tremendous cultural turmoil among the Indians. They debated the necessity of uprooting their families from centuries-old homelands and relocating to the west. One Alabama story from this time depicted a berdache (a European designation for an Indian homosexual or transvestite)[60] urging a group not to leave. He stated that there was plenty of game remaining in the region and that he would not run from the advancing Europeans; instead, he would hide under a bed, stab as many of them as possible, and die for his actions. Unconvinced, the group left, traveling by river west through Choctaw country. The narrative also relates the manner by which the Europeans had previously obtained Alabama land: "They would get the Indians drunk, and when they had become sober they would find bags of money hung to their necks in payment for land."[61] Hard liquor was quickly accepted and has played a major role in Alabama-Coushatta culture since its introduction.

The westward migration of some Alabama and Coushatta contingents (along with a group of their Pakana Muskogee relatives) began in 1764 with their relocation to Bayou Manchac on the English east bank of the Mississippi River, about ten miles south of present Baton Rouge, Louisiana.[62] Ethnographer Howard Martin suggests that they descended the Alabama River to Mobile, traveled along the coasts of Alabama and Mississippi, across Lake Pontchartrain and Lake Maurepas, up the Amite River, and over the Manchac or Iberville River to the Mississippi River.[63]

Responding in the 1780s to the rapid growth of English settler population, some of the Alabamas began moving into Spanish Louisiana. One village was established in Opelousas District and another on Bayou Boeuf. The Coushatta also relocated to Louisiana, where they, under the leadership of Chief Red Shoes, built a settlement on the Red River, sixty miles north of its mouth.[64]

Even though the Alabamas and Coushattas were in Spanish territory, English traders continued to supply them with English goods. Spanish Lt. Gov. Joseph de la Peña reported in September, 1772, that the "English maintain themselves in Los Apeluzas with such audacity as to have said to Joanis not only that they would trade there but that they would go where they pleased. On the other hand, they supply in El Rapide the Aliba amon [Alabama] nation of that place." De la Peña complains that these goods are traded from one Indian nation to another, "and thus they will introduce their trade among these nations of the interior."[65] English cultural influence would remain important in the Alabama-Coushatta community until it was supplanted by American political and social cultural forces.

In 1800 Napoleon secured the Treaty of San Ildefonso, secretly transferring Louisiana back to the French, who unexpectedly offered to sell all of the Louisiana Province to the United States. At a cost of four cents per acre, the 1803 Louisiana Purchase included territory extending from Canada to the Gulf of Mexico and west to the Rocky Mountains. Native Americans were not consulted regarding the transfer of title of their land; the Alabama and Coushatta towns now stood in U.S. territory.

The United States desperately needed information about its new land and inhabitants. In December, 1803, William C. C. Claiborne, Territorial Governor, assumed control of Indian affairs, and Dr. John Sibley was appointed Indian agent for the tribes west of the Mississippi River. The new agency was established at Natchitoches.[66] This initiated the period of direct cultural influence on the Alabama-Coushattas by the United States federal government.

Sibley soon began sending reports back to Washington. His 1806 report described a forty-year-old Alabama settlement in Grant Parish. He stated that the Coushatta arrived in 1796 at Appelousa and moved in 1802 to a site eighty miles south of Natchitoches on the Sabine River. There they numbered about two hundred men.[67] The Freeman-Custis expedition reached another Coushatta village on the Red River, one hundred miles north of Natchitoches.[68]

The tribes had maintained their previous patterns of settlement of widely dispersed homesteads clustered around a small town.

Coushatta bands continued to leave their homes on the Alabama River for the west. Before 1809 they had established two villages on the Red River, the lower being nine miles northwest of the present day Coushatta, Louisiana.[69] In 1807 the lower village was abandoned after an incident that illustrates the deeply entrenched cultural practice of retribution: A Coushatta man was killed in self-defense by a white man. Sibley promised the victim's family that the killer would be tried, but after five months nothing had been done, and in retaliation a white man was killed by a young Indian named Siache. Several months later four Alabamas killed a white inhabitant of Opelousas, also apparently in response to the Coushatta man's death. When Sibley requested that Siache be handed over, the Coushatta refused his admonition, and the entire town moved into Spanish Texas.[70] The Alabamas, however, cooperated with white authorities, and the four murderers were quickly arrested. Two were pardoned and two hanged on August 3, 1808.[71]

These incidents are important illustrations of both the transition and retention of custom. The family of the murdered Coushatta was willing to put aside the law of retaliation and allow American justice to settle the matter. When that system proved essentially ineffective, retaliation was effected at the cost of a life and a communal migration. The Alabamas allowed the white legal system to conclude the matter, but the Coushattas relocated instead of acquiescing to white legal and cultural expectations.

By 1805 the Alabamas had settlements on the Angelina River, Attoyac Bayou, and the Neches River. A combined population of Alabamas and Coushattas in 1809 within seventy miles of Nacogdoches was estimated to be 1,650 people.[72]

For thirty-seven years Texas had been an internal section of Spanish territory, when in 1800 its eastern border became the international boundary. The United States' acquisition of Louisiana in 1803 made Texas critical to preventing American expansion into New Spain. Spanish governors hoped that the various Indian groups would function as a buffer between themselves and the Americans, but they could never be completely confident of allegiances. In 1817 Antonio Martinez, the last Spanish governor of

Texas, "ordered" the Coushattas to attack a band of encroaching Americans, but he also felt it necessary to warn the Indians not to assist the intruders.[73] This incident suggests that Spain assumed a political and military hegemony over the tribes that was marginal at best.

In 1821 a coalition of conservative elites, the Catholic clergy, and liberals declared and received Mexican independence. That same year Moses Austin was granted permission to establish a colony of three hundred families in Mexican Texas.[74] This ushered in the period of rapid Anglo movement into the territory. Mexican officials also courted the Indians along the eastern border. In a move designed to secure title to specific property, Alabamas, Coushattas, and Cherokees were granted the right to petition through an attorney. The tribes were apparently willing to utilize this culturally specific mechanism, but they could not afford to hire a lawyer.[75] This illustrates a longstanding phenomenon among many Indian nations. Cultural transition had proceeded to the point at which non-Indian cultural expressions (legal mechanisms) were accepted, but the Indians did not possess the resources to utilize those cultural artifacts.

In 1830 Alabama Indians lived in three communities in what became Tyler County, Texas. The largest town was Peachtree Village, followed by Fenced-In Village and Cane Island Village. Peachtree Village was located on the Alabama and Coushatta Traces, and it was the terminus for Long King's Trace.[76] The majority of the approximately six hundred East Texas Coushattas lived in three towns: Long King's Village, Battise Village, and the Lower Coushatta Village (Chief Colita's home).[77]

By 1835 a diverse group of insurgents had decided that a Texas war for independence was their only option. The Alabamas and Coushattas remained neutral during this conflict, although their assistance of fugitives in the 1836 "Runaway Scrape" has been retained in the popular memory.[78]

In 1836 Sam Houston, representing a temporary Texas government, negotiated a treaty with the Cherokees and "Associated Bands." This vague and somewhat ethnocentric designation included the Alabamas and Coushattas. Later, in 1837 the Senate of the new Republic of Texas failed to ratify the treaty, which would have provided a large land grant north of the old San Antonio Road.[79]

Houston was succeeded as Texas president by Mirabeau B. Lamar, who established a very different relationship with Texas Indians, one characterized by expulsion and extermination. On July 9, 1839, Lamar wrote letters to Chief Colita and the Coushattas and to the white citizens of Liberty County, encouraging both groups to refrain from harassing the other. In his letter to the whites he explained that the Coushattas were weak and defenseless, but that it would be unwise to provoke them into joining with stronger, more aggressive tribes.[80] Lamar's policy of expulsion caused much conflict along the border with Indian Territory to the north, as displaced Cherokees and others mounted raids into Texas.[81] Some of the Coushattas joined in the anti-Texan activities, raiding and then retreating north across the international border. This prompted some whites to declare in May, 1842, that Texas and the Coushattas were (briefly) in a state of war.[82]

In 1840 the Republic of Texas legislature authorized two leagues of land for the "benefit and use" of the Alabamas and two leagues for the Coushattas.[83] When surveyed in 1844, the tract was found to be claimed by Hamilton Washington. He agreed to allow the Indians to remain on the land; Battise Village was occupied entirely by whites who refused to give up the territory. The land designated for Alabamas was also occupied by whites,[84] and subsequently the grants became ineffective and were negated.[85]

After Texas was admitted to the United States in 1845, control of Indian affairs became a divisive issue. In most newly admitted states the federal government owned land that could be used for reservations. In Texas, however, at the time of admission all land belonged to either the state or to private owners. Eventually, the state made some land available for federally supervised Indian reservations along the Brazos River.[86] Although other Indians were to be sent to federal reservations, the Alabamas and Coushattas remained under the jurisdiction of the Texas government.

In 1854 the Alabamas received a grant of 1,280 acres in Polk County from the Texas legislature.[87] The following year the Coushattas received a grant of 640 acres, but once again, the land was already occupied by whites. Most of the Coushattas drifted back to the Coushatta Village near Kinder, Louisiana, and in 1859 the Alabamas allowed the remainder to join them on their reservation. The surrounding non-Indian community frequently failed to distinguish between the two tribes, and referred to the reservation residents as "our Indians," Alabama-Coushattas, or "Polk County Indians." While distinctions and tribal affiliation remained clear to the Indians themselves, intermarriage increased significantly, and movement toward a shared identity began.

The greatest cultural transformation during this time resulted from political restructuring as relations with the Creek confederacy were severed. During the migration period the chief, or chiefs, retained his (their) position of leadership. Presumably, councils of second men and elders also continued to advise them. The records give no evidence of "war" and "peace," or "red" and "white" towns. Abandoning the Creek Confederacy and its related social/military influence probably ended the need and the opportunity afforded by the red/white system.

Towns and villages continued to be built on navigable river sites in proximity to tillable land. Since the busk continued to be celebrated and stickball played, the basic configuration of round house, town square, and ball field was retained.

The housing unit remained the log cabin, usually clumped in small groups of three or four. Botanist Jean Louis Berlandier claimed that a Coushatta homesite was virtually identical with that of a white settler. There were "fowls in the yard and stores set aside."[88] Sheep were raised and corn was cultivated as a cash crop.[89] Part of what Berlandier attributes to white acculturation were traditional Alabama-Coushatta lifeways, such as the cabin design and the general configuration of the site. Other skills such as the husbandry of chickens, hogs, and sheep were acquired from whites.

Lino Sánchez y Tapia accompanied Berlandier and provided illustrations of various Indians. He depicted two Coushatta men wearing red turbans and short hair. They both sport ear ornaments, and one wears a nose ring. One dresses in buckskin shirt, leggings, and high-topped moccasins; the other wears blue cloth shirt, greatcoat, buckskin leggings with red garters, and low-cut moccasins. Each wears a red sash and carries a long-barreled rifle.[90] These fashions demonstrate strong European influence, particularly in the choice of cloth.

Military organization continued to revolve around the small, mobile raiding party. As illustrated by Sánchez y Tapia's depiction of Coushattas with rifles and metal tomahawks, lithic weapons and tools had by the nineteenth century been replaced to varying degrees by metal blades and firearms.[91]

Maize remained the primary crop, with watermelon,[92] sheep, and chickens being added to the former list of auxiliary produce and livestock. American- or European-manufactured tools were utilized whenever possible. The Texas Indian Bureau provided the Alabamas and Coushattas with farm implements, as demonstrated by a January, 1845, account statement that included shipping from Galveston to "Elis" landing. The list of supplies included blankets, stroud cloth, axes, hoes, saws, a pipe hatchet, harnesses, and plows.[93]

Although Berlandier referred to the Coushatta penalties of death and mutilation for adultery, he stated that there was no need to exercise them. Either he was misinformed, or there was a tremendous attitudinal change since the time, less than a century previously, when the penalty for adultery had to be altered to preclude the loss of a majority of warriors. He also stated that they were monogamous, which, if true, would mean that polygyny had been largely abandoned. Continued and increased contact with European practices regarding monogamy, and the fear of incurring shame, might have caused the decline of this practice. It is more probable, however, that he was misinformed. Examples of polygyny among the Alabama-Coushattas exist well into the twentieth century.

The busk continued to be celebrated, although perhaps in a modified form. The black drink was still utilized, as was a general purification and cleansing. There is nothing to indicate that essential theological perspectives were modified or that there was any conversion to Christianity.

One element of personal identity was in transition during this period, as the Alabamas and Coushattas began to assume European surnames. Tribal members working for non-Indians were given the name of the property owner. This led to examples of parents and their children, and of siblings, possessing different surnames because they did not have the same employer.[94]

Although some Alabamas remained in their ancestral home, and some eventually migrated to Oklahoma, contact with these groups was minimal at best. The situation is similar for the

Coushatta, except that many remained in western Louisiana, and some of those in Texas returned to the Louisiana Coushatta communities, the largest and most permanent being near Kinder, Louisiana. The Texas and Louisiana communities have maintained close social contact since the migration period.[95]

External forces introduced by Europeans included disease, military and political interaction, and other cultural practices relating to agriculture, technology, sexual values, and language. These stimuli mobilized internal forces for survival. When the majority of a town was killed by disease, remnants moved in with other Indians. When geographic political and military hegemony shifted from one European power to another, whole towns relocated. When more productive agricultural or technological practices were introduced, they were incorporated. What was not dramatically altered was religious belief and practice. The busk and other festivals were celebrated long after migrating west. Life still followed an agricultural and hunting cycle. Traditional athletics were pursued in conjunction with festivals. Relationship with deity remained rooted in the necessity for purification and its availability.

This cultural continuity persisted in the Texas Alabama-Coushatta community until the latter part of the nineteenth century because the Alabama-Coushattas were geographically isolated from external forces. New stimuli for cultural change were introduced to the tribes in the 1880s by Presbyterian missionaries. While earlier contact with Catholic missionaries had produced no converts, the Presbyterians achieved virtually complete conversion in a generation. Their efforts in education, religion, and health care inaugurated a period of cultural transition unprecedented in Alabama-Coushatta history.

CHAPTER 3

"Fields White Unto Harvest"

Governments and Missionaries, 1854–1930

*Go ye therefore, and teach all nations, baptizing
them in the name of the Father, and of the Son, and
of the Holy Ghost: Teaching them to observe all things
whatsoever I have commanded you: and, lo, I am
with you alway, even unto the end of the world.*
—*Jesus of Nazareth*
Matthew 28: 19–20

*I have nothing against Christ, I just wish he
would come and talk to the Indians and leave
the missionaries at home.*
—*Benji Benally, Dine'*

Personal identity is rooted in culture. Someone introducing himself as Alabama or Koasati (Coushatta) in 1880 possessed a set of
cultural features that separated him from other groups, including
language, attire, religious beliefs, recreational and athletic pursuits, roles and responsibilities within the community, sexual relationships, health care procedures, funerary practices, and, perhaps,
physical appearance. Two generations later, someone identifying
herself as Alabama-Coushatta was clearly distinguishable from the
surrounding community only by language and, possibly, physical
appearance. By 1930 virtually all other cultural representations were

surrendered or were in an advanced state of transition. This change in culture caused a concomitant shift in personal identity.

Those external forces exacting the greatest cultural change in the Native American community were the United States government and Christian missionaries. During three centuries of contact with whites, the Alabama-Coushattas experienced significant transition as European and American political and military pressure caused them to leave their ancestral homes, migrate west, and settle on a small reservation in east Texas.

Although their lives were disrupted and altered during this migration period, much traditional culture remained. Abba Mikko was acknowledged, purification rites were practiced, dances were held, and stickball was played. Even laboring on local white plantations and participating in the Civil War did not end these practices. Most significantly, three centuries of contact with governments and government agents did not destroy the sense of community. This, however, was accomplished by Presbyterian missionaries in less than half a century.

Cultural transition that resulted from contact with federal and state governments was not extensive during this period. There was some intercourse with whites through the state-appointed agent and through military service during the Civil War. More significant to cultural change was off-reservation employment and trade. It is illustrative to examine briefly these contacts to provide a contrast with subsequent federal and state intervention.

Interaction with the state of Texas was limited during the early reservation period, although the government did attempt to implement a relocation scheme four years after the Alabamas moved on to the reservation in 1854. In May, 1858, James Barclay was appointed as Indian Agent in Polk and Tyler Counties by Gov. H. R. Runnels.[1] One of his first assignments was to persuade the hesitant Polk County Indians to move to a reservation on the Brazos River.[2] There they would receive an "abundance" of good land and regular support from the state.[3] Barclay was instructed to take some of the tribe's leaders to the proposed site, and if they consented to the removal, to consolidate the various Indian bands for a peaceful and expeditious emigration.[4] This proposed removal would have increased Indian dependence on the state, altering economic and cultural identity.

The federal government, with state approval, had created two reservations on the Brazos River in 1854. Approximately twelve hundred Caddos, Anadarkos, Ionies, Wacos, Kichais, Tawakonis and Tonkawas were assigned to the Brazos Reserve. The Clear Creek Reserve was for the Penateka Comanches. Before plans for the Alabama-Coushatta removal could proceed, however, a group of white Americans attacked and massacred a group of Indian men, women, and children on the Brazos River Lower Reserve, the proposed site. This was done in retaliation for attacks by nonreservation Comanches in West Texas.[5]

Fearful that it could no longer protect its Indian wards from unruly whites, the state subsequently closed the two federal reservations in 1859, sent the inhabitants to Indian Territory, and abandoned the proposed Alabama-Coushatta resettlement program. Governor Runnels told Barclay that the Alabama-Coushattas should not be sent "where they might at any time be indiscriminately slaughtered, for no other cause than that the Creator has made them Indians."[6]

Principal Chief Antone and subchiefs Cilistine, Thompson, and John Scott had a letter drafted and sent to Sam Houston in December, 1859. In it they requested to remain on their reservation. They said they were comfortable and had "plenty of corn, and potatoes and have many hogs, and cattle, and horses." The chiefs estimated their population to be five hundred Alabamas and two to three hundred "Cashattees." The letter writer, H. C. Pedigo, included an addendum describing the Indians as "good and worthy men," who "live comfortably, and have in abundance the necessities of life."[7] Apparently, in 1859 there was no immediate threat to survival to provide opportunity for dramatic cultural change. It also suggests the degree of cultural transition in material resources, such as the use of horses, cattle and swine.

The first opportunity for cultural mutation caused by daily contact with non-Indians came four years later during the Civil War. A few of the Polk County Indians served briefly in Capt. Charles Bullock's Company G, 24th Texas Cavalry, in 1862,[8] but by the end of that year they had returned to their homes.[9] The following year the Texas Transportation Corps of Engineers (Beazley's Cavalry Company) was created to protect the Trinity River, the most navigable waterway in Texas. Indians built snag-boats that were placed as obstructions in the river.[10] The Alabama and Coushatta soldiers participated in no major battles of the Civil War, but significantly large sections of the tribe were exposed to white culture on an intimate, day-to-day basis. Nevertheless, the only evidence of possible internal transition is the adoption of the surname "Bullock" by some Indian families.

Increased non-Indian influence was proposed in 1866 by Gov. James W. Throckmorton of Texas, who requested that the U.S. government appoint an agent for the Alabamas and Coushattas and provide them with "a few gifts."[11] Federal officials, however, were in turmoil over proposed Indian policy. Lewis Vital Bogey assumed the reins of the Bureau of Indian Affairs on November 1, 1866,[12] and he fought for control of Indian affairs to remain in civilian hands. This alienated him from many in the Senate who wanted to see a military hegemony established. His appointment was never confirmed, and Rev. Nathaniel Taylor became Commissioner of Indian Affairs in 1867, reiterating the relationship between church and government in Indian affairs.[13] Taylor's successor in 1869 was Ely Samuel Parker, a Seneca Indian. Loyal supporter of Gen. Ulysses S. Grant, Parker advocated military supervision of Indian affairs.[14] During his tenure the Alabamas and Coushattas were placed under federal military jurisdiction in 1870, although no agent was appointed for them.[15]

A U.S. investigator, Capt. Samuel Whitside, was sent to the Texas tribes in 1869. Impressed with the Alabamas, Coushattas, and their close neighbors, the more assimilated Pakana Muskogees, he recommended that the post commander at Fort Livingston be appointed as the Indians' agent. The government once again failed to act on the suggestion.[16] Thus, the tribes not only postponed but evaded significant direct cultural influence by the federal government.

The Alabama-Coushattas remained virtually untouched by federal and state policy for the remainder of the nineteenth century. During the last decades of the century and into the twentieth century, consistent attempts were made by attorney J. C. Feagin in lobbying the federal government for more Indian land. Although no direct action resulted, Feagin's actions brought the tribe to the attention of Congress.[17]

In 1910 the Department of the Interior investigated Alabama-

Coushatta living conditions. This report showed the people to be living in log cabins with rudimentary furniture. Diet was reportedly limited almost exclusively to corn dishes.[18]

Nothing resulted immediately from this survey, but in 1918 the Secretary of the Interior recommended an appropriation of $100,000 for land purchases and $25,000 for livestock and agricultural equipment.[19] The resulting appropriation of only $8,000 was targeted, instead, for education. Some $5,000 was designated for construction of a small schoolhouse, $2,000 for land purchases, and $1,000 for additional information gathering. An appropriation of ten cents per day per student was also included.[20] At this time education on the reservation was being directed by Presbyterian missionaries.

A reminder of the low status of Indian identity within the larger cultural context of the United States occurred early in this century. Military involvement was honored by Alabama-Coushatta people, whose traditions stretched from the Civil War back into the precontact past. When World War One erupted, one half of the adult males in the tribe volunteered for military service. Six men served in the conflict,[21] but the majority were rejected because they were Indians.[22]

Nonreligious outside influence came not only from federal and state officials but from local whites, who sometimes exerted pressure on both the tribe and the government. The reservation could have lost 192 acres of timberland in the 1920s because a surveyor failed to file his field notes with the General Land Office when the reservation was initially established. The property subsequently came into the possession of the Kirby Land Company, where W. E. Merrem, a young attorney and later vice president of the East Texas Pulp and Paper Company, discovered the error after his employment by the company in 1921.

One of Merrem's family traditions was that the Alabama-Coushattas had helped his grandmother and her children during the Texas Revolution. He decided to return the favor. He had the original survey filed and dropped the lumber company's claim. Merrem toured the reservation with Sunkee Mikko (Chief Sunkee) and suggested to him that the reservation boundary be fenced to help avoid future disputes.[23]

Another local non-Indian exerted much greater influence on

the tribe, and ultimately, on the state and federal governments. Livingston attorney Clem Fain, Jr., became interested in the reservation Indians and attempted to generate interest in the reservation among the surrounding community. In 1927 the state sent several senators and guests on a fact-finding mission to the reservation,[24] and in 1928 Fain organized a group of Livingston citizens to press the state legislature to create the position of agent, to which post he was appointed. Fain then engaged the cooperation of the Texas Federation of Women's Clubs, who helped organize a delegation, including Sunkee Mikko, to go to Washington, D.C.

In the capital the delegation appeared before the Congressional committee on Indian Affairs. In his report Assistant Commissioner of Indian Affairs Marritt stated: "It is my opinion that if the American government owes anything to any Indians it is to the Alabama-Coushatti of Texas."[25] The delegates also visited the Smithsonian Institution and met with Pres. Calvin Coolidge.

The group's efforts were rewarded with an appropriation of $40,000. Additional land was purchased with $29,000 of the federal funds, bringing the reservation's holdings to 4,315 acres.[26] The following year a Texas Senate Special Committee recommended that $110,000 be appropriated for the tribe.[27] In 1929 Texas made an additional appropriation of $47,000 that was in part designated for the construction of a gymnasium, hospital, and agent's house.[28]

The influence of these nonreligious external forces was primarily limited to land and material acquisitions. The tribe had previously experienced numerous relocations and long-term contact with whites without loss of traditional religious beliefs and practices. Self-imposed confinement on the reservation in conjunction with intensive Presbyterian missionary efforts during the last decades of the nineteenth century elicited unprecedented cultural changes. The impact of their efforts far outweighed the results of contact with federal and state officials and policies. Their actions and motives were completely consistent with other similarly engaged religious workers and with Euro-American society as a whole.

The religious trends becoming evident on the Alabama-Coushatta reservation at the end of the nineteenth century had begun a century earlier. Fervor associated with the "Second Great

Awakening" among American Protestants caused the creation of eleven mission societies between 1787 and 1820.[29] The sole aim of these entities was to be culture brokers: convert and civilize the Indians.

Civilizing the Indian meant dismantling existing cultures and rebuilding them in the white American mold. According to historian Robert F. Berkhofer, Jr., "civilization as conceived by Americans in this period meant an upward unilinear development of human society with the United States near the pinnacle."[30] Those who held to this tenet believed that, blessed by God, Euro-Americans had the obligation to reach down to their less fortunate brethren. Minister Bruce Kinney wrote in the early twentieth century:

> That is also the measure of our obligation to the Indians. It is a case of *noblesse oblige*. It is the obligation that the strong owe to the weak; that the educated owe to the ignorant; that the rich owe to the poor; that the wise owe to the superstitious; that the free owe to those who are in bondage and that every Christian owes to every heathen.[31]

Indians were savable, according to Rev. Issac Whittmore, who wrote in 1893 that it required much force and determination:

> This influence (the church) on a people just emerging from heathenism and breaking up old superstitions and vices, and instead of them, leading an industrious and virtuous life, must far exceed that of churches in town on a civilized people.[32]

Charles Cook, Methodist-turned-Presbyterian missionary to the Pimas, paid his own way to Arizona soon after the Civil War, where he taught and preached. For him, Indians and non-Indians had "a great privilege [of being] invited to walk with God."[33] The manner of that walk, however, was strictly circumscribed.

Responses to the external force of the missionary and his message were as varied as the culture and languages of the numerous Indian nations. Some, like the Pueblos in 1598, 1680, and 1695, resisted violently the imposition of new cultural expressions. Others attempted to incorporate some Christian teachings in a syncretic religious expression or millenialist cult, represented by Paiute visionary Wovoka's "ghost dance." Many Indians came to believe, like Beverly Hungry Wolf, Blackfoot, that Indians had no future unless the old ways were put aside.[34]

Education became the tool used most effectively by culture brokers. It was hoped that the hearts and minds of the young could be molded to accept and internalize the values of the external culture. Resettlement to a reservation, it was believed, helped missionaries focus young minds on the task at hand. Indian Commissioner William Medill suggested that these "colonies," a "temporary expedient," would help "civilize" the Indians by protecting them from unsavory white influences, and would teach them to become farmers. Missions would be opened where schools could instill the Protestant work ethic.[35]

The common cause of the two great external forces, government and church, achieved its greatest cooperation in the period of Pres. Ulysses S. Grant's Peace Policy, 1869–82. During this time numerous mission schools were begun as seventy reservations came under direct missionary control.[36]

Indian emphasis on community was the greatest obstacle faced by the missionaries. Historian William G. McLaughlin describes the cultural distinction: "Christianity, in its American form, was based on a competitive, materialistic, aggressive ethic completely at odds with everything in the corporate, communal religion of the Indians." Conversion was the measure of success, and according to Berkhofer, "true Indian conversion meant nothing less than a total transformation of native existence."[37]

Indian religion had met the needs of people for thousands of years, and only weak communities were very susceptible to the Christian message.[38] Missionary education, therefore, attempted to undermine and weaken Indian culture through instruction of the children in three areas: religious, vocational, and academic. In each of these, emphasis could be placed on the individual rather than on the community.[39] Former Cherokee Chief Wilma Mankiller describes early mission schools among the Cherokees as places where, in an attempt to "save the savages, . . . academic lessons were supplemented with an abundance of hymn singing, public prayers, and Scripture reading."[40]

The last two decades of the nineteenth century witnessed dramatic cultural and economic change on the Alabama-Coushatta reservation as a result of new employment and religious influences. In 1875 the Houston East & West Texas Railroad was organized, and it reached Polk County in 1881. More significantly, Presbyterian missionaries arrived in 1880 and began intensive proselytizing efforts. The impact of their presence was a complete transformation of Alabama-Coushatta identity.

The arrival of the railroad opened new employment possibilities for the Indians in logging, lumber, and related industries.[41] Numerous Indians were soon employed by the lumber companies, which were willing to hire as many as desired to work.[42] The purpose of some cultural artifacts is not always obvious in other cultural contexts: the Indians were unsure of the purpose of the first coins they received, and the oldest living resident of the reservation, Jimmy Johnson, remembers many of them being drilled and made into jewelry.[43]

Coushattas in Louisiana heard from their Texas relatives about the employment possibility and came to live near the reservation in lumber camps. Coushatta elder Ludie Battise traveled to Texas with her family when she was about four years old (in the 1920s), her feet hanging off the side of the flatbed railroad car. She adds that they brought their house with them.[44] In fact, the lumber camps consisted of box cars that had been converted to homes and offices. The railroad track ran between them and constituted the camp's main street.

The lumber camp closest to the reservation and the site of most Indian employment was Camp Ruby. Dedie Williams, Alabama-Coushatta tribal elder, worked there as a young girl, clearing trees and brush for horse and oxen lots and maintaining roads. With her pay of "three-something" a day, she and other Indian youth purchased horses that they rode to and from work. Rain did not slow work at the multiracial camp that consisted of Indian, white, black, and Mexican workers.[45] Perhaps the greatest impact on identity resulting from this experience was the close proximity of other cultures. This was a period of considerable miscegenation.[46]

More important to cultural transition was the establishment of a Presbyterian Church on the reservation in November, 1880.[47] When the first Presbyterian minister arrived on the reservation around 1878, there were no Christians. In 1884 the church was inaugurated with fourteen charter members. When Rev. and Mrs.

Chambers arrived on the reservation in 1889, they found all the Indians, except for one man, to be church members.[48] This mass conversion was made possible by several cultural factors, the most critical being the necessity of developing survival strategies.

Circumstances surrounding the coming of the missionaries have achieved somewhat mythic status on the reservation. Tribal memory states that immediately prior to the Presbyterians' arrival, Joseph K. Sylestine was born to an Alabama-Coushatta mother and a white father. His mother died, and Joseph was raised in his father's home, where he learned English. He eventually returned to the reservation to live.[49]

Several years later, Rev. S. F. Tenney, pastor of the Crockett Presbyterian Church, was on his way to Beaumont when he became lost and sat down in the snow. An Indian from the reservation found the minister and offered to take him to the nearby Indian village.[50] There the English-speaking young man welcomed Tenney to his home and invited him to remain as long as he desired. He stayed several days and then left with Indian escorts, who accompanied him some distance toward Beaumont.[51] After Rev. Tenney's visit, Rev. Thomas Ward White was asked by the Presbyterians to preach to the Indians. While at the reservation, he also provided a Christmas tree and many gifts collected from churches around the country.[52]

In April, 1880, Dr. Tenney, who had been so moved by the Indian hospitality, suggested that the feasibility of securing a missionary for the reservation be explored by the Eastern Texas Presbytery. In November of that year Dr. L. W. Currie and his wife were employed and dispatched to the reservation's 250 inhabitants. Chief John Scott supported the missionaries' initial efforts, and a few converts were made. In 1883 a log cabin school was built and classes were begun. Though it was more for his teaching than for his preaching that Dr. Currie was remembered by the Indians,[53] a church with fourteen charter members was established in 1884.[54]

Some members of the surrounding non-Indian community were not pleased with the missionaries' efforts, and the log cabin church-school was burned by whites in 1886.[55] The Indians' corn and livestock were also pilfered by local whites.[56] Walter Broemer, reservation superintendent during the mid-twentieth century, states that the local farmers in the nineteenth and early twentieth centuries exploited Indian labor and feared that the status quo would be altered through the missionaries' efforts at education and Christianization.[57]

These non-Indians pressured the Curries into leaving the reservation in November, 1886, and they moved to Alaska to continue as missionaries to Alaskan natives. Mrs. Currie returned to the reservation upon the death of her husband in 1890, and she taught school there until her retirement in 1900.[58]

The church was served by various guest ministers for an interlude, and then Rev. W. A. Jones filled the pulpit from 1890 to 1897, followed by Rev. W. C. Tenney in 1898.[59] In 1899 Rev. Caleb W. Chambers and his wife Emma moved to the reservation. They remained for thirty-seven years.[60]

The transformation from the Southeastern cultural complex's theological system, which had existed in dynamic form for at least a millennium, to Reformed Calvinist Christianity was accomplished in less than two decades. Several factors contributed to this phenomenon. First was the similarity in the two cosmologies, a consideration to which most contemporaneous white observers were blind. Vine Deloria, Jr., historian and Native American, states that Indian and Christian ideas were never in confrontation, but that "rites and techniques" were frequently the subject of conflict.[61] Alabama-Coushatta tribal member Joe John relates that he was told as a young man that conversion was accomplished rapidly because the two belief systems were so similar.[62]

Mrs. Nettie McClamroch, non-Indian historian and activist at the Indian Presbyterian Mission, expressed the widespread belief that the Alabamas and Coushattas "had no idea of God."[63] According to Zetha Battise, educator and former Alabama-Coushatta Tribal Council member, the missionaries did not recognize that they and the Indians already worshiped the same Creator.[64] Wilma Mankiller, longtime principal chief of the Cherokee Nation of Oklahoma, explains that the Cherokees, bearers of similar cultural and theological traditions as the Alabama-Coushattas, frequently embraced Christianity without surrendering traditional beliefs. Today, many Cherokees practice the old ways at home and in ceremonies and also attend church on Sunday.[65]

Similarities in the theological systems include the belief in a supreme creator deity, the need for purification and its availability, the awareness of a pantheon of minor supernatural beings (angels, demons, spirits), a commitment to prayer and supplication as a means of communicating with deity, a belief in an afterlife, common worship and celebration through ceremony and festivals, and the conviction of the possibility of supernatural and divine intervention in human lives. Therefore, it is not a great leap from the intoxicating purification celebration of the busk to the assurance of rebirth symbolized in baptism and the communion cup.

Christmas and Easter replaced indigenous festivals. For many Indians, angels and demons now walked where spirits and "the little people" had before. Prayer was now to Jehovah rather than to Abba Mikko. Conversion, however, was more semantic than ideological because the new religious system fulfilled the same social-psychological role as the old.

One major contrast with European Christianity was that Indian religion emphasized personal action rather than assertion of creeds. Revelations were experienced during times of fasting, sacrificing, and private visions. Indian religion was individual in origin and social in impact. It defined actions in this world rather than emphasizing salvation in the next.[66]

Similarity in the theological systems is not, however, a motive for change. The single greatest catalyst for conversion was the pursuit of physical and economic survival. During the last quarter of the nineteenth century the reservation was plagued with tuberculosis, pneumonia, and malaria,[67] combining to reduce the population by 35 to 40 percent.[68] This familiar reduction of native population by disease challenged the traditional medical-religious system.[69] The Alabama-Coushattas adjudged their medicine people to have been the most powerful of any tribe,[70] yet their cures proved ineffective against these foreign maladies, and his or her influence was undermined at the same time in which the missionaries were vigorously proselytizing. Their words and medicines offered hope when traditional practices failed.

Another element of survival was spiritually based. The missionaries instilled fear through their promulgation of the doctrines of hell, damnation, and the devil. Jack Battise explains that "we had never heard of anything like the devil. We knew there was evil, but we never gave it a name."[71] According to Jack Battise's wife, Lawrine Low Battise, people were extremely afraid of going to hell,[72] rather than to the traditional afterlife land in the West.

Local economic and cultural conditions, such as the hostility of local whites and competition for jobs, gave urgency to the missionaries' message of change. Joe John, reservation resident and former Assembly of God minister, states that "we were told that we had to become white in order to survive," at least insofar as possible. This meant learning a new language, becoming literate, and adopting a new religion. "Now, we don't remember what we used to believe."[73]

Four factors contributed to enhancing the credibility and power of the missionaries' message. Traditional religious leaders held a high social position in Native American society, and this esteem was often accorded to Christian ministers. Thus, Dr. Tenney and the other missionaries were made welcome. There was also an ethnic hierarchical dynamic at work that accorded the missionaries power. Author I. A. Coston claims that the Alabama-Coushatta possessed a "strange social code," which they "believe and practice, 'the white man first, the Indian next, the dog next, and the negro next.'"[74]

A third factor was the ethnic-specific, and from the white perspective, excessive response to kindness and generosity. A Euro-American anonymous observer who associated closely with the tribe in the mid-nineteenth century stated that "to one from whom they have uniformly received (kindness) and in whose truth and justice (they) have confidence, they will yield up their own will entirely, and become as facile in his hands as a child."[75] In discussing the Indian attitude toward missionaries and the phenomenon of conversion, Walter Broemer, former reservation superintendent, explains that the Alabama-Coushatta will typically do whatever they are asked to do by a white person in authority.[76]

A fourth source of credibility and impetus to change was the support of the chief. John Scott, chief for forty years until his death in 1913, assisted the missionary endeavors.[77] Three elements combined to produce the virtually universal conversion of the Alabama-Coushattas to Christianity by 1899: The perception that change was necessary for survival, the elevated status of the missionaries, because of their race, profession, and chief's support, and the ethnic tendency toward easy manipulation by friends.

Missionaries stripped away cultural expression and living religion, replacing these with Western European creeds. According to Vine Deloria, Jr., salvation was measured by the successful regurgitation of the Catechism, the Nicene Creed, and the Apostle's Creed. The primary message of the missionaries "sought to invalidate the totality of Indian life and replace it with Christian values." The living daily reality of Indian religion was replaced with preaching and teaching "words and phrases."[78]

Church membership did not necessarily mean conversion to the extent the missionaries expected. Delores Poncho, Dine' and resident-through-marriage of the Alabama-Coushatta reservation, explains that Christianity has many definitions and expressions. The Alabama-Coushattas retained many of the old ways while embracing a limited number of the missionaries' teachings.

While traditional beliefs were not completely eradicated, erosion of the community ethic contributed significantly to a transformed identity.[79] People began developing individual survival strategies rather than those designed to strengthen the community. Every facet of life, including health, education, and religion, was addressed by missionaries promoting the cultural value of individual aggrandizement and accomplishment.

When the missionaries arrived in the 1880s, they found an essentially intact indigenous culture. Despite three hundred years of contact with non-Indians, Alabama-Coushatta society retained much of the old belief system.[80] The universe contained the seen and the unseen, with which humans frequently interacted. Abba Mikko, the Sky Chief, was the supreme deity. Medicine men and witches communicated with, and influenced, the supernatural. Witches were greatly feared; one young Alabama girl, Emily Sylestine, related in 1932 that two witches had been executed by the tribe as late as the 1880s.[81] Dedie Williams remembers her mother's story of those deaths: One man had tried to escape by climbing up to his roof, but he was dragged down and killed.[82]

The general emotional state or average disposition of Alabama and Coushatta individuals was also noted by early observers. In 1861 a longtime friend of the tribes, a person fluent in their language, described them as "a very happy people," who were "warm hearted and cheerful."[83]

People believed that if the green corn ceremony were ever suspended the crops would fail.[84] According to Jack Battise, retired auto mechanic and Alabama-Coushatta medicine man, the "stomp" dance arena was well maintained and often utilized. The dances subsequently ended through missionary influence. The Indians also played *tele,* Indian stickball, on a large field with goals at each end. There were few rules in the game, and it often became very rough.[85]

The Indians raised hogs and cattle and cultivated corn, sweet potatoes, vegetables, and fruit trees. Supplementing their resources by hiring out as contract labor to local plantations, Indian cotton pickers easily found employment because of their nimble fingers.[86] The Alabama-Coushatta loved to hunt, and, after the harvest was completed, the men took their families on annual hunting trips for deer (for meat and pelts), and bear (for oil.)[87]

Although they retained some traditional attire, much had already been adopted from the whites. One observer at mid-century described "a troop of Alabamas, riding through the town with baskets and dressed deer-skins for sale. They were decked with feathers, and dressed more showily than the Choctaws, but in calico: and over their heads, on horseback—curious progress of manners—all carried open black cotton *umbrellas.*"[88]

The sense of community remained strong, with the Indians distributing their available resources as needed among themselves and among their guests. Children were especially prized, and if a child were orphaned, there would frequently be a contest to determine which family would adopt the boy or girl.[89] Commitment to the well-being of the community remained the greatest social value.

The primary efforts of Rev. and Mrs. Chambers in transforming Indian culture were in the fields of proselytizing, education, and medicine. The ultimate purpose of nineteenth-century Protestant missionaries was well expressed by a white observer at the Tucson Indian School, who described the chief aim being "to introduce the leaven of the Gospel, not a gospel of words, but a gospel that produces regeneration of heart and character in the individual, which makes men and women careful, industrious, and pure, useful members of the family, the community and the state."[90]

Rev. Chambers preached at church services three Sundays a month on the reservation, serving another church on the fourth. His time was spent conducting Presbyterian Church Session meetings, prayer services, counseling, and visiting in the homes of the Indians.[91]

With traditional medical practices increasingly disparaged and undermined by missionary teaching, and apparently ineffectual during the epidemics, the Indians turned to the missionaries for medical help. Dr. F. J. Hart described how his influence grew among the Papagoes in Arizona: "During my first few weeks here I was looked upon with suspicion by the Indians, and closely watched. It came about that the wife of the chief was taken violently ill, and I was called to attend her. The nature of the case was such that I gave immediate relief. This gained the respect of the chief, which has continued to grow. Being in the chief's favor all were soon friendly to me."[92]

Rev. Chambers also began to offer health care. He enrolled in a nursing course and also requested and received assistance from Polk County physicians. One surgeon invited him to observe in the operating room. During this period the severity of malaria and the frequency of pneumonia-related deaths were somewhat reduced.[93] The increasing role of non-Indian health care providers successfully compromised the cultural emphasis on community by challenging common beliefs in the efficacy of traditional medicine and by undermining the authority of longstanding community leaders.

In November, 1926, State Health Officer Dr. James C. Anderson summoned the medical doctors and dentists to the reservation for a clinic. One hundred and seventy-nine Indians were examined (88 adults, 57 school children, and 34 preschool age children), and 95 percent had "very bad teeth and gums." The physicians found heart problems and "numerous complaints of rheumatism and kidney trouble," along with many cases of poor hearing, poor vision, and infected eyelids. There was a surprising amount of obesity, which the doctors attributed to an imbalanced diet. Infant mortality was extremely high.[94] These illnesses and their treatment by non-Indians contributed to the growing reliance on white medical practices.

The reservation school also provided indoctrination to white ways. Mrs. Chambers began teaching school in 1900 and remained until 1937. The curriculum included elements of Indian education found in Indian schools across the country: religion, vocational training, and western-European-derived academic courses. Each of these areas emphasized the importance of the individual and, correspondingly, devalued the Indian community.

Mrs. Chambers bought readers for the students, who ranged widely in age. Mcconnaco Battise began school at the age of twenty-seven, and Bronson Cooper Sylestine, later to become chief, started at age twenty-one. Mrs. Chambers' first goal was to teach English to the Indians. The process of civilizing the Indian required a significant command of this language.[95] She found a guide for teaching English to European immigrants in Boston, and she employed the same method with her students.

Participation in non-Indian athletic activities grew and increasingly disrupted older cultural ideology by bringing the Indians into immediate contact with non-Indian culture. Mrs. Chambers described her students as being "very good in handwriting and drawing," and stated that basketball had become the favorite sport of both boys and girls.[96] This assertion indicates that disruption of traditional Indian athletic and recreational activities was successful after a generation of missionary presence. Eula Battise, tribal elder, played marbles in the 1920s with "store-bought" marbles, which were a source of pride.[97]

Extended hunting trips in autumn were no longer taken, and white American games rapidly replaced traditional Indian activities. Jimmy Johnson recalls two forms of the Indian stickball sport, *tele,* when he was young: the traditional version, played on a large field with goals at each end, and the later form, with a single thirty-foot pole at the center of an arena.[98] Jack Battise also remembers his parents playing *tele.* In another version of this game men competed against women in attempting to throw a leather-covered ball with sufficient accuracy to hit a small platform or target placed atop a thirty-foot pole. Men held a short hickory stick, *kapochee,* in each hand, while women used their bare hands. Each stickball stick was about eighteen inches long; extending from one end was a strip of hickory, bent over and secured with leather strips to form a small cup or basket at the end.[99] Dedie Williams also played *tele* with *kapochee* as a child, but by the time she was in high school in the 1930s, playing basketball outside the senior high school building had replaced the traditional Indian sport.[100]

Another internal response to external forces relating to recreation was the adoption of winter games called *olinway*. The name itself of this December activity was possibly a corruption of the English "runs all the way" because participants were expected to run during the entire activity.[101] The seven-day celebration took place in the evenings during the week between Christmas and New Year's Day. Three or four large bonfires were built around a field or yard, providing light for the participants. Adults ranging in age from older youth through elders engaged in a variety of Euro-American children's games. After playing for some time at one house, the participants moved to another home on the reservation to repeat the revelry.[102]

The children loved to sing, and Mrs. Chambers frequently sang to them and had them sing their school lessons.[103] Memorization of scripture was a significant portion of the curriculum.[104] The mixture of religious instruction with academic pursuits was never questioned, allowing individual-oriented religious belief to be introduced to children at an early age.

In 1922 there were 47 "scholastics" enrolled in the seven-grade school. All students took classes in arithmetic, reading, spelling, and writing. Some also studied history, composition, grammar, and drawing during the five-month school session.[105] In the 1931–32 school year the Indian village school had 65 primary level students and 15 high school students. Adults became convinced of the necessity for Euro-American education. Three of the seventh graders were twenty-one years old and 11 of the high school students were eighteen or older. By that time the term had increased to 160 school days.[106] White education with its concomitant values was insinuating itself into daily life to a consistently greater degree.

Two years later there were seventy-four students, of whom only three, (tenth graders) were over seventeen. All elementary students took arithmetic, government, language, music, nature study, physiology and hygiene, physical education, reading, spelling, and writing. The library held sixty volumes, thirty elementary level and thirty secondary level.[107] The Indian village school was made an independent school district in 1934,[108] and by the 1940s everyone between nine and forty years of age was literate.[109] One Indian woman, Mrs. Lizzie Sylestine, received some training and began teaching at the reservation school in 1932.[110] After sixty years of missionary presence, sermons, and education, traditional Alabama-Coushatta religious belief and cultural practice was virtually nonevident.

Specific cultural representations that underwent transition during this time illustrate a significant movement away from Indian communal values to white cultural expectations. Jimmy Johnson (born 1906) remembers his father wearing a buckskin "breechclout" and "leggins," and the women wearing buckskin dresses.[111] As an integral expression of Native American culture, attire was a symbol of the struggle between old and new. Changes in Indian clothing were considered important enough to report in mission publications, as exemplified by Rev. C. H. Cook's statement in *Presbyterian Home Missions* regarding Pima women in 1882: "Our meetings are well attended; a number of Indian women in this neighborhood come, wearing dresses like their white sisters."[112]

Alabama-Coushatta buckskin dresses were soon replaced by long-sleeved, ankle-length black dresses that conformed to white expectations.[113] Men wore their hair and beards long until given the utensils and instructions for haircuts and shaves by white men early in this century.[114] Short hair on men became the accepted standard for the next half-century.

Jimmy Johnson also recalls that Indians continued to adopt European surnames based on the identity of their employer. This practice could lead to a confusing family tree. His father worked for a family named Johnson, and soon he became known as Johnson. Jimmy's paternal uncle was employed by the Lockharts and appropriated that surname.[115] The replacement of Indian names with European names is indicative of the transformation of personal identity during this period.

Diet consisted of "fry bread" or biscuits, corn dishes like *yukchee* and *sofkee,* supplemented with beef and pork, and with wild game such as squirrel, rabbit, turtle, robins, opossum, raccoons, and fish.[116] Venison was eaten when available, but most of the deer had been hunted out of east Texas by non-Indians. People often ate with a knife as the primary utensil, but missionary influence soon established the use of a fork. Bread was used to push food onto the knife and into the mouth. Coffee was poured into the saucer to cool and then to drink. After a satisfying dish or entire meal, an oral expression of approval, an exhaled "uh," was given.[117]

Until the 1940s people walked or rode horses. Trips to local stores were taken with horse- or oxen-drawn sleds or travois, with which to carry home groceries and other purchased items.[118] As white culture made inroads, trains and automobiles became more prevalent. Because of a car's limited carrying capacity, automobile usage encouraged emphasis on the individual rather than the community. Except when a bus was available, people did not travel in large groups, and their opportunity for social interaction was therefore limited.

Homes continued to be geographically dispersed, much as they had been for hundreds of years. Spacious two- and three-room log cabins, with earth or wood floors and large hearths for cooking and heating, were common throughout the reservation. Although the new frame homes continued the old homestead pattern, their construction encouraged movement away from the community ethic. Instead of being erected by the community in a joint activity that reinforced a sense of mutual dependence, the new homes were built by outside contractors and funded by the government.

Houses erected in 1930 through appropriation financing were built to government specifications, with smaller rooms and a small cookstove. Many Indians felt this was a step backward from their older homes, and some refused to move into the new homes.[119]

These homesteads with their adjacent gardens were tied together with a network of forest trails.[120] Zetha Battise remembers numerous evening meetings that concluded with the visitors making their way toward home in different directions from her house. Each person carried a torch consisting of a long sliver of turpentine-rich pine pith, leaving a stream of illumination visible along the forest trails.[121] This vivid cultural artifact diminished as the practices of walking to destinations and visitations ceased.

In the heat of a still summer night, families would often sleep on the porch to take advantage of what little breeze was available.[122] When it was cool enough to sleep inside, soft, warm mattresses of moss were used. After the moss became flattened through the weight of its occupant, it was simply replaced. Floors were swept with brooms made of long grasses, and the sandy yard was hoed frequently. Water came from fresh springs.[123] During this period factory-produced mattresses and brooms became available, and people drilled water wells. Again, Indian cultural expressions were replaced with non-Indian practices.

In the late evening parents related tribal beliefs and traditions and told stories about the spirits that remained on the reservation.[124] Yards were kept devoid of grass because spirits will not cross the open sand or dirt.[125] This landscaping practice could sometimes get a child into trouble, because parents recognized their children's footprints. Ludie Battise remembers when one child received a new pair of shoes and was instructed not to wear them while playing around the house. The child disobeyed, leaving telltale tracks to and from the creek, of which her parents took ample note and action.[126] The practice of removing grass ended during this period, as missionary attacks on belief in the supernatural were overtly accommodated, if not universally internalized.

Although the clan system was maintained, its impact was limited primarily to prohibition of same-clan marriages.[127] The old tradition of cutting a baby's hair at four months was also retained and practiced, although no one remembered its origin or exact purpose. In this ceremony two men placed the baby on a bearskin rug and cut his or her hair, possibly symbolizing a new and healthy beginning in life.[128]

The coming of the missionaries and Christianity affected many areas. Berkhofer suggests that the two most frequent causes for suspension of church privileges were intemperance and adultery.[129] This was certainly the case for the Alabama-Coushattas. The Presbyterian Church Session minutes indicate frequent appearances by young women confessing to the sin of adultery. One young woman appeared before the session in August, 1910, with her illegitimate child. After expressing "hearty repentance [*sic*]" she was suspended for a year from "the ordinances of the Church. This action was taken especially in view of warning others of the young people of the congregation."[130]

The traditional practice of polygyny was continued until the early twentieth century, with Chief Thompson, Sunkee Mikko, reportedly having two wives.[131] There are no further references to multiple concurrent spouses.

Much traditional belief was retained early in this period relating to burial ceremonies. In order to keep unwanted spirits from lingering, the house of the deceased was scrubbed from ceiling to floor as part of a purification rite. Clothing worn to the funeral was removed before entering one's home.[132] Items of particular importance to the deceased were placed on top of the grave, although the purpose for this custom was forgotten. These cultural expressions gave way to white funerary practices. Burial sites were moved from the individual homestead to a centralized cemetery. Non-Indian style coffins were manufactured and later purchased from outside sources. Funeral services were held in the church and conducted by a minister.

Tribal leadership was increasingly undermined. The last "traditional" leader, Chief John Scott, was born about 1806 and lived until March 3, 1913. His first wife refused to accompany him to the reservation when it became available, and his second wife, a Caddo Indian, was 105 years old when he died.[133] Scott encouraged the missionary presence during the period of epidemics and aided them in establishing a church.

There was a fifteen-year period after John Scott's death during which the tribe had no official chief. This would not have been possible in an earlier period, but the tribe had come to depend on non-Indians for leadership. Chief Charley Thompson, Sunkee Mikko, was inaugurated on January 21, 1928, and served until his death in 1935, at which time Bronson Cooper Sylestine was elected. He died in 1970.[134]

The Alabamas and Coushattas entered the reservation with much of their traditional culture intact. They interacted with the surrounding white community on a limited basis, through employment, military service during the Civil War, and infrequent intermarriage. These contacts did not compel extensive internal cultural transition.

The arrival of the Presbyterian missionaries in 1880, with the subsequent introduction of the concept of a vengeful God, compelled a dramatic change in religious and cultural practices. Many tribes experienced a division into traditional and Christian factions, but the Alabama-Coushatta embraced the new religion *en masse*. Well-intentioned missionaries ushered in an era of cultural transition in areas including religious belief, language, attire, recreation, employment, and medicine. These individuals were perceived by non-Indians to be saviors of the tribe. At the centennial celebration held on the reservation on January 1, 1936, Judge E. T. Murphy stated that Rev. and Mrs. Chambers were "in a large measure responsible for the existence of the Alabama-Coushattas. Without the devoted care which they have given to the Indians, it is doubtful if the tribe could have continued to survive."[135]

Although the cultural transformation appeared virtually all-encompassing to non-Indian observers, remnants of traditional beliefs and practices remained. Many of these were challenged in the following decades, but the undercurrent remained strong.

These cultural transformations caused a dramatic transition in personal identity. Being Alabama-Coushatta in 1930 meant something very different from being Alabama or Koasati (Coushatta) two generations earlier. Remaining cultural distinctions disappeared almost completely during the next two generations. The missionaries continued to exert pressure for change, but their preeminence as culture agents was supplanted by federal and state intervention through new legislation (the 1930s Indian New Deal and the 1950s termination of federal responsibilities) and through participation in two wars. Throughout the decades from 1930 to 1960 Alabama-Coushatta identity continued down the path of assimilation. Surviving vestiges of medicine and other cultural artifacts were forced underground, to be practiced covertly by a few elders.

Chief Colabe, 1780–1864, Mikko from 1806–64.
Courtesy Alabama-Coushatta Indian Reservation

Chief John Scott (Ta-Faloke), *1805–1913, Mikko from 1871–1913.*
Courtesy Alabama-Coushatta Indian Reservation

Chief Charles Martin Thompson (Sunkee), 1860–1935, Mikko from 1928–35.
Courtesy Alabama-Coushatta Indian Reservation

Chief Bronson Cooper Sylestine (Ticaiche), *1879–1969, Mikko Choba from 1936–69.*
Courtesy Alabama-Coushatta Indian Reservation

*"Happy New Year" in the Alabamo language, January 1, 1970 inauguration
of Chief Robert Fulton Battise (Kina), 1909–94, Mikko Choba from 1970–94,
with* (left to right) *Sharon Sue Poncho, Arvelia Battise, and Jack Battise, Sr.
Courtesy Walt and Frances Broemer*

*"Fancy" dancer Douglas Williams, Jr., in powwow regalia accompanied
on drum by Jack Battise, Sr., in the tribal tourist complex, ca. 1972.
Courtesy Walt and Frances Broemer*

Chief William Clayton Sylestine (Oscola), *b. 1932, Mikko Choba from 1995.*
Courtesy Alabama-Coushatta Indian Reservation

Delores Poncho (Dine'), *Tribal librarian, and Roland Poncho, Tribal Council chairman. Courtesy Alabama-Coushatta Indian Reservation*

Indian Presbyterian Church on site of former dance arena.

*Frances and Walt Broemer, former Texas Indian commissioner and Alabama-
Coushatta Reservation superintendent. Courtesy Walt and Frances Broemer*

*Jeanine Polite, the first girl to make two thousand career points
at Big Sandy High School, Homecoming, January 24, 1997, with*
(left to right) *Coach Andy Snider, Maxine Polite* (mother),
and Ardie Polite (father). *Courtesy Lydia Morris*

Jo Ann Battise, Alabama-Coushatta tribal administrator.
Courtesy Alabama-Coushatta Indian Reservation

CHAPTER 4

Three Decades
of Government Paternalism,
1930–60

*If our culture is dissolved, Indian people as such
will cease to exist. By definition, the causing
of any culture to cease to exist is an act of genocide.*
—*Russell Means,
Indian Activist*

During the first half-century of Presbyterian missionary presence among the tribe, Alabama-Coushatta culture and identity was transformed. By 1930 the majority was literate in English, which was read and spoken in church and school. Basketball was the preferred sport. Attire emulated non-Indians with whom the Alabama-Coushattas worked in rice fields and lumber towns. It was similar to that of the "poorest class of whites," with numerous patches on their overalls indicating both "poverty and thrift." Each Christmas the Indians received packages of used clothing from other Presbyterian congregations.[1] Forgotten were the green corn ceremony, the stomp dance, and the old songs.[2] To be Alabama-Coushatta was to be Christian in the Calvinist tradition. The cultural stage was set for the entrance of that other great culture broker in Indian history: government. After 1930 the mantle of the most influential change agent shifted from the church to the federal and state legislatures, which had played only a minor role to this point.

The greatest cultural influences of the three decades from 1930 to 1960 resulted directly and indirectly from federal and state initiatives. In 1929 federal appropriations allowed the purchase of additional land and the construction of frame homes. Concomitantly, the state of Texas assumed increasing control of the reservation school, which was eventually phased out during the 1940s. In response to passage of the 1934 Indian Reorganization Act, the tribe incorporated, drafted a constitution, and elected a Tribal Council. When World War Two began, many men from the reservation enlisted. Their exposure to, and interaction with, non-Indian cultures had a profound effect upon them and on the post-war reservation.

During the early 1950s the United States government initiated a termination of federal trust responsibilities with many tribes, including the Alabama-Coushattas. Although most of the tribes' financial support was already being received from the state of Texas, termination also transferred land management, education, and health responsibilities to state auspices. Perhaps the greatest impact of the termination process was to demonstrate the coercive nature of federal policy in blatant disregard of tribal practices. Cultural hegemony was virtually all-encompassing as the federal government, using its agent as a culture broker, imposed western political expectations.

A mass-media culture broker was introduced to the reservation during the 1950s by Rev. William Albert Smith, who became minister of the Presbyterian Church in 1952. Smith purchased a television, put it out on his lawn, and invited people to sit around and watch.[3] Soon, several Indian families purchased televisions and invited others over to watch in their yards as well. Fry bread and drinks were sold, and the most popular programs were boxing and wrestling.[4]

As people gathered outside the Presbyterian minister's manse to watch the new device, they viewed a world very different from their own. Reservation resident Joe John suggests that television was influential because it publicized the availability and desirability of an extensive variety of material goods then unknown to the Indian community.[5] Yet to a non-Indian observer visiting the reservation in the late 1950s, the Indians on that lawn might not have appeared much different from the rest of American society. They wore the same clothes, studied the same subjects in school, and prayed in a Presbyterian Church indistinguishable from any suburban Protestant church. Their skins were darker than most whites, and the older ones spoke an Indian language. Essentially, however, they were fully assimilated.

The new cultural influences of federal and state government introduced during this period, combined with the missionaries' continuing efforts as cultural change agents, led to increasingly "Europeanized" culture and revised personal identity. Concern over loss of language and traditional skills grew toward the end of the tri-decade, and coincided with the introduction of the tourist industry, leading toward the creation of a supratribal identity and nascent efforts at ethnogenesis. Prior to 1929 the Alabama-Coushattas were essentially isolated from government intervention. Subsequently, however, they found themselves directly and indirectly affected by federal and state actions, and therefore, they continually re-evaluated their cultural and personal identity.

The origins of increased federal and state intervention are found 150 years earlier as the nascent United States attempted to develop an official policy for dealing with Indians. It is illustrative to depict briefly this evolving federal-Indian relationship. The Articles of Confederation drafted by the American colonists, effective 1781, made the government of the new United States the "sole and exclusive" authority over Indian affairs.[6]

Initially, the United States recognized Native American nations as distinct political entities. The Constitution granted Congress the power to "regulate Commerce with foreign Nations, and among the several States, and with the Indian Tribes."[7] Early United States Indian law and policy was determined by federal legislation and by Supreme Court decisions. Under provisions of the Indian Trade and Intercourse Acts, 1790–1834, virtually all official interaction between Indians and non-Indians was placed under federal jurisdiction. The intent of the legislation was to protect Indian territorial integrity, control disposition of Indian land, regulate trade with Indians (especially liquor distribution), provide for prosecution of interracial crimes, and encourage assimilation into white society.[8] From this point onward, forced assimilation would be a favorite policy, one which by definition meant the negation of native culture and the ascendancy of Euro-American values and practices.

From its inception until 1871 the United States negotiated formal treaties with the various and distinct Indian nations. These treaties established the basic facets of federal Indian law, including the trust relationship, the sovereignty of Indian nations, the reserved rights doctrine, and Congressional plenary power in Indian-related legislation.

In *Cherokee Nation v. Georgia* (1831) Chief Justice John Marshall opined that Indian tribes could "be denominated *domestic dependent nations*"[9] (my italics), and in *Worcester v. Georgia* (1832) he stated "that a weaker power does not surrender its independence—its right to self-government, by associating with a stronger, and taking its protection."[10] This opinion set the precedent for tribal sovereignty and for a trust relationship that is usually described as one of ward and guardian. With this political status came the concomitant paternalistic implications for the eradication of Native American culture, ideas that were so vigorously pursued by missionaries.

Subsequent to the Removal Act of 1830 most of the southeastern tribes were cajoled or coerced into migrating across the Mississippi River to Indian Territory. These nations, including the so-called "five civilized tribes," Cherokee, Choctaw, Chickasaw, Creek, and Seminole, had already experienced significant cultural transformation, adopting white forms of government, law, economy, religion, and education. The greater the degree of surrender of traditional culture and emulation of European values, the more "civilized" they became. Being "civilized," however, could not prevent their forced removal, which ripped at the hearts of peoples whose identity was vested in the land.

During Andrew Jackson's administration 100 million acres of Indian land east of the Mississippi was obtained through almost seventy treaties. This territory cost the government about $68 million and 32 million acres across the river. The Mississippi River became the new dividing line between white settlement and Indian territory.

Between 1845 and 1848 the United States expanded territorially through the acquisition of Texas (1845), the Oregon country

(1846), and the Mexican Cession, which included California (1848). Soon, white Americans were crossing Indian lands in great numbers and encountering a whole new group of Native Americans— the Plains nations—who resisted the loss of their land and other material and spiritual resources.

To address the new Indian problem, Indian Commissioner William Medill, a devout assimilationist, suggested in an 1848 report that two large reservations be created. These "colonies," a "temporary expedient," would help to "civilize" the Indians by protecting them from unsavory white influences and teaching them to become farmers. Missions would be opened, and schools could instill the Protestant work ethic.[11] The reservation system was inaugurated with one of its stated purposes being the manipulation and eradication of native culture. From its inception, the stated purpose of the reservation system was cultural genocide.

During the next four decades more and more reservations were increasingly created by statute and executive order. Land was obtained through treaties in accordance with precedent set in the East during the later colonial period and by the young United States: Negotiate from a position of power and coerce a lucrative settlement. The reservation system was designed to accomplish two objectives, namely, to make more land available to white settlement and to provide an environment that forced assimilation.[12]

In 1887 the General Allotment Act (the Dawes Act or Severalty Act) was passed, authorizing the allocation of land parcels to individual tribal members. Its implementation reduced Indian landholding from 138 million acres in 1887 to 48 million acres in 1934.[13] Family heads received 160 acres and single persons received 80 acres.[14] Missionaries, educators, and some politicians had pursued a policy of forced assimilation for several centuries: The Indian must be made to adopt white values, or he would never become a viable part of United States society. This objective was at the heart of the Dawes Act, as Senator Dawes himself articulated: "The head chief told us that there was not a family in that whole [Indian] Nation that had not a home of its own. There was not a pauper in that Nation, and the Nation did not owe a dollar. It built its own capitol . . . and it built its schools and its hospitals. Yet the effect of the system was apparent. They have got as far as they can go, because they own their land in common. . . . There is no enterprise to make your home any better than that of your neighbors. There is no selfishness, which is at the bottom of civilization."[15]

According to historian and Native American Vine Deloria, Jr., substantive change in Indian policy came not with the Dawes Act itself but with 1891 amendment to the act. The amendment shifted the intent from one of educating Indians in how to manage private property as part of the assimilation process, to one of designating the federal government as determiner of how an Indian's allotment of land was to be used. It "empowered the Bureau of Indian Affairs to act in place of the aged, the young, and the mentally infirm Indians in the use of their property."[16] The Severalty Act unilaterally forced U.S. citizenship, and also, for the first time, introduced the criteria of "blood quantum" in identifying Native Americans.[17] This physiological measurement of inclusion in Indian communities would become the most divisive issue in Native American communities.

In 1924 the Indian Citizenship Act was passed, and all Indians who had not become U.S. citizens through the General Allotment Act and other procedures were made citizens, whether or not they desired that legal status. Some Indian nations, such as the Six Nations Iroquois Confederacy, immediately challenged forced citizenship.[18]

The Brookings Institution prepared the Meriam Report in 1928, detailing deplorable living conditions on many reservations. Stripped of cultural and material resources through the Dawes Act, Indians struggled for survival. The Meriam Report recommended that funding for health programs and education be increased, that self-government be facilitated, and that the allotment process be ended. The report was strongly supported by non-Indian reform groups such as the Indian Rights Association.[19] No longer a widespread threat through warfare or economic competition, Indians were encouraged to take steps toward cultural reaffirmation and regeneration.

Congress responded to the Meriam Report by passing the Indian Reorganization Act (the Wheeler-Howard Act or Indian New Deal) in 1934. This legislation attempted to stabilize tribal landholding by suspending allotments and subsequent land sales. It also sought to foster tribal self-governance through encouraging the development of Tribal Councils, tribal constitutions, and tribal corporate charters that would exclude or replace existing political structures.[20] Many tribes were suspicious of any federal Indian policy and were especially dubious of an externally imposed form of governance. Tribes were given two years to debate acceptance or rejection of the Indian Reorganization Act, at which time 181 tribes voted for acceptance of the Act, and 77 voted against.[21]

Commissioner John Collier's Indian New Deal promoted the establishment of tribal councils intended to interface with the Bureau of Indian Affairs. According to Collier, the Indian Reorganization Act had two purposes: "conservation of the biological Indian and of Indian cultures," and "conservation of the Indian's natural resources."[22]

In response to Washington's initiative, the Alabama-Coushatta drafted a constitution that established the criteria for tribal membership at 100 percent Indian blood quantum.[23] This stipulation for tribal membership, and therefore for personal identity, further undermined the traditional concept of inclusion through participation in the community. One was now Alabama-Coushatta (legally designated as a single tribe) because he or she could prove a specified physiological status rather than through personal and communal ascription. This furthered the process, introduced by the missionaries, of transferring the focus of identity away from the community and to the individual. The constitution also provided for the creation and continuation of a Tribal Council comprising seven members with the chief (mikko) serving as adviser and tie-breaker.[24] Traditionally, however, leadership was vested primarily in the mikko with advice from the clan elders. By this time, the white presence had undermined tradition, and important decisions were being made by agents and missionaries. The Alabama-Coushatta Tribal Council soon fell into disuse, to be revived two decades later. The council was essentially irrelevant in dealing with the federal government during the 1930s and 1940s because there was limited contact between the two entities. The superintendents of the Alabama-Coushatta reservation from 1928 to 1950, under the auspices of the Texas Board of Control, were Clem Fain, Hobby Galloway, Ralph Howe, J. E. Farley, Rex Corley, and J. B. Randolph.[25] These men were the Indians' point of contact with both state and federal governments.

The only consistent and personal interface between the Alabama-Coushatta and government was in the area of education. Missionaries began teaching English in 1884, and an eight-grade school was established on the reservation, but Indian languages were still spoken in the home and to peers. Language, the most visible cultural tie to the past, was the one element most directly challenged during this period. Although children were being taught English in school from the turn of the century, Albamu and Koasati were spoken at home. Special Commissioner Nash noted in 1931 that the greatest defect of the reservation school system was the limited contact with white students, resulting in "an exceedingly poor command of spoken English."[26]

The Indian village school was organized as Common District 17 of Polk County, with a 1932 appropriation of $15,000. The school board at the time was composed of Ed Battise, Bronson Cooper Sylestine, and Jeff Battise. The faculty comprised Mr. J. P. Galloway (principal), Mrs. Chambers, Miss Lillian Thomason, and Miss Lizzie Battise, who received a combined annual salary of $545.[27] In official records the Indians were counted with white students, but on the "Head Teacher or Principal's Term Report" for 1931–32 "Indian" is handwritten over the "white-colored" category. In that year there were eighty students, with none in the tenth or eleventh grades (there was no twelfth grade).[28]

The Indian school on the reservation was the sole institution in the independent school district in 1934.[29] After the retirement of Mrs. Chambers, teachers at the school included Herman H. Fitzgerald (principal and coach), Mrs. Herman Fitzgerald, and Lizzie Sylestine, a reservation resident who by 1940 had completed three years of college, a strong indicator of acculturation.[30]

In 1944 students above grade three were transferred to Big Sandy school.[31] The next year the reservation school closed, and all of the 106 students were transferred to other districts, primarily to Big Sandy.[32]

Although the number of enrolled students increased steadily during this period, those actually attending decreased. During the 1944–45 school year the enrollment indicated 103 scholastics, but only 66 attended. Educator Willie King suggests three explanatory factors for the situation: difficulty in locating and keeping qualified teachers, basketball being dropped from interscholastic competition, and increased availability of wartime jobs for older students.[33]

Andrew Battise and other tribal leaders were concerned about the decline. They believed that by transferring their children to white schools the trend could be reversed. "We do not want a separate school for our children. We want our children to attend the white schools."[34] The missionary efforts at cultural transformation were effective, and the impetus to "become white" was strong. This would conceivably lead to better education, better jobs, better leadership. In short, it meant survival.

In 1946 when the reservation school was closed, students were forced to attend non-Indian schools. Here they encountered social and educational settings where they were punished for speaking their first languages. Although an Indian woman, Cora Sylestine, taught the first three grades at Big Sandy, she did not allow students to speak their Indian language. Current Tribal Administrator Jo Ann Battise remembers being punished for speaking her first language by being forced to sit on a chair placed on top of the teacher's desk.[35] Children were coerced into speaking English from age six, and they engaged in classroom and athletic activities with white students where only English was spoken. The ascendancy of the Alabama-Coushatta language on the reservation declined from this point.

At the end of the 1950s an English kindergarten was established, to be followed by a "Headstart" program. Children were forced to learn and use English at progressively earlier ages. Mastery of English was critical in another arena: the military. It was during service in World War Two that many Alabama-Coushatta men developed a better command of spoken English. They also learned much about non-Indian culture.

World War Two was a period of identity transition for many Indians. According to Indian Commissioner William A. Brophy, "the war caused the greatest disruption of Indian life since the beginning of the reservation era."[36] A higher percentage of Native Americans served in the war than any other minority group. Twenty-five thousand Indians served in the military, and forty thousand Indian wage earners relocated to cities during the war. Two American Indians were awarded the Congressional Medal of Honor, and the Navajo "code talkers" gained national recognition.

The war represented an impetus to assimilate even before men and women enlisted. Knowledge of English was a prerequisite for military service, and many Dine' volunteers, for example, were rejected because they were unable to speak it. This created a sudden demand for education on their reservation, eventually leading to the formation of the Navajo Community College.[37]

The war experience was a culture shock for Indians coming from rural Indian communities and reservations. The high-paced materialistic culture proved attractive to some, and this made the transition back to reservation life extremely difficult. Ira Hayes is the most visible example of this identity dilemma. After being honored and feted for his role in raising the flag on Iwo Jima, this Pima Indian returned to his reservation in Arizona. Selected to represent the tribe in Washington, Ira was overwhelmed by the bureaucracy and failed to accomplish tribal objectives. He returned to the reservation briefly, then went to work in Chicago for the Indian Bureau's relocation program. Plagued by continuing publicity of his struggle with alcoholism, Ira again returned to his reservation. He died there in January 1955 of exposure and alcoholism.[38]

Native Americans returning from the war effort frequently found themselves estranged from their traditional communities. Rituals were conducted to decontaminate and purify some of the returning warriors. The Dine' held "enemy way," or "squaw dance" ceremonies to restore balance to the veterans' lives.[39]

Post-war reservations offered limited employment options to the returning veterans, and many viewed the reservation as a halfway house between military service and assimilation in the non-Indian community.[40] The increasing economic pressure forced many to migrate to urban areas. In mainstream society mixed-bloods with fewer Native American physiological characteristics were accorded greater social equality than full bloods. To avoid discrimination, many mixed-bloods began denying their Indian ancestry and created a non-Indian identity. Colloquially, they were able to "pass."

World War Two service had another effect on Indian identity. Prior to the war most reservation Indians had experienced little contact with Native Americans from other tribes. Their lives revolved around their family and their local community, with only limited exposure to other tribal beliefs and practices. Personal identity was rooted in tribal identity. With military service, however, Indians of all tribes were grouped together and identified simply as Indian. Men and women from diverse tribes found comfort in their shared experiences, and this provided a precedent for the subsequent development of supratribal identity and activities, particularly in the urban context.

Many veterans remained only briefly on the reservations after the war, then migrated to cities in search of work.[41] The pattern of discomfort upon returning to the postwar reservation is evident among the Alabama-Coushattas. When war erupted, many men in the tribe volunteered and served with distinction. Soon after his induction Daniel Battise was wounded and returned to the reservation. Subsequent to his recuperation, he reenlisted and served in the Atlantic and Pacific, from Alaska to Africa, with a unit that was the forerunner of the Special Forces Green Berets. At war's end he returned to the reservation briefly, married, and moved to Chicago, where he remained until retirement in 1995.[42]

Other Alabama-Coushatta veterans, like Mark Sylestine, decided to make the military their career. When Mark left the reservation and went to Oklahoma in the late 1930s, his only oral command of English was "yes" and "no." Subsequent to being drafted in 1942 at the age of twenty-one, he served in the Army Air Corps in Europe. At the end of the war Mark decided to retain the sure income provided by a military career. He later retired, married an Oklahoma Cherokee woman and eventually moved back to the reservation in 1979.[43]

Men who were uncomfortable with reservation life upon their return from military service sometimes became change agents themselves. Emmett Battise saw active duty as a staff sergeant in Italy. He became accustomed to giving orders and found it difficult to readjust to civilian life. Subsequent to his discharge he remained on the reservation less than a year and then enrolled at Stephen F. Austin State University in Nacogdoches, Texas. He was later elected as second chief and returned to the reservation.[44]

Tribal elders Lawrine Low Battise and Dedie Williams view the wartime experience as the inauguration of a modern period of increased alcoholism and family disintegration.[45] These trends accelerated during the following decades.

The federal government, influenced by Native American participation in the war and by mixed-blood de-Indianization, concluded that assimilation was being accomplished and moved to absolve itself of trust responsibilities. In the postwar atmosphere of virulent anticommunism, government control and Indian Reorganization Act services on reservations smacked of socialism.[46] In his 1946 "Aspects of Indian Policy" report to Congress, President Harry Truman, concerned with the bureaucratic excesses of the Bureau of Indian Affairs, called for its elimination within three years.[47] "Progressive" full bloods and mixed-bloods, particularly ex-servicemen, called for more individual incentives such as education assistance, personal loans, and a reduction in federal involvement at the tribal level.

The impact of termination on most tribes was immediate and pervasive. One hundred and nine cases of termination were processed between 1945 and 1960, affecting 1,369,000 acres of Indian land; after this period more than one-half of the U.S. Indian population resided in urban areas.[48] This urban migration coincided with growing civil rights activity and political awareness in other ethnic communities and contributed to the development of supra-tribal consciousness and the pan-Indian powwow phenomenon.

John Collier resigned from the Bureau of Indian Affairs in 1945, and his successor, William A. Brophy, initiated dramatic new policies. Brophy believed that Indian veterans were ready to assimilate with the dominant non-Indian society. A means of facilitating that assimilation was the creation in 1946 of the Indian Claims Commission, which existed until 1978 when it was dissolved by Congress. The goal in establishing the Claims Commission was to conclude all outstanding obligations to Indians. The expected cash settlements would allow tribes to become independent of federal assistance and involvement, and would permanently end federal responsibilities. Title to large tracts of Indian lands was retroactively transferred to the United States, and frequently the Indians were forced to settle for a pittance of the land's actual value.[49]

Immediately after the creation of the Claims Commission a series of new bills aimed at the complete emancipation of the Indian and at a dramatic reduction in federal services. On February 8, 1947, William Zimmerman, Brophy's successor, presented to Congress a blueprint for termination policy. He separated U.S. tribes into three categories based on his perception of their readiness for removal from federal trust status. Consistent with the Zimmerman Plan initiative, the House of Representatives in 1947 decreased appropriations to the Bureau of Indian Affairs by 50 percent. Schools were slated for closing, and hospital budgets were slashed. On August 4, 1947, Congress passed House Resolution 3064, removing the Laguna Band of Mission Indians in California from the federal trust relationship. Amid the funding cuts, Alaska Natives, Dine' and Hopis received increased federal support.

Termination of federal trust responsibilities meant that tribal land was divided and distributed as allotments to individual tribal members. Many were unable to derive revenues or sustenance from their plots and were forced to sell the land. Some tribes resisted termination through all available legal channels. The Montana Blackfeet and Pine Ridge Oglala Lakota, acting on the advice of their attorney, physically blocked Bureau of Indian Affairs impoundment of their tribal headquarters. The government labeled this ultimately successful action as "Communist inspired."[50]

In March, 1950, President Truman announced the appointment of Dillon S. Myer as Indian commissioner, and John Nichols dutifully submitted his resignation. As director of the War Relocation Authority Myer had overseen the removal of Japanese-Americans from the Pacific coast during World War Two. He thoroughly opposed Collier's policies and immediately discharged BIA officials who held views similar to those of the former commissioner. Myer suggested that in order for the Indian to break free from the cycles of despair and paternalism, they must have industrial training programs. He believed that the Indian's relationship with tribal land was flawed because it had not allowed the Indian to meet white expectations. Indian culture had not been adequately extinguished and replaced with white values. The relationship therefore needed to be terminated.[51]

Myer was passionate in his determination to dissolve the Bureau of Indian Affairs, which he believed would liberate Native Americans to enjoy fully United States citizenship. John Collier criticized Myer for turning the Bureau into an instrument committed solely to termination.[52] Myer's hard-line attitude alienated many tribes. They feared that termination could be a threat to their traditional life-ways.

On June 30, 1953, the Department of the Interior reported that tribes in Oregon, California, Minnesota, and the Alabama-Coushatta of Texas had approved termination of federal supervision. In July, 1953, Congress approved House Concurrent Resolution 108, initiating a termination policy that lasted into the early 1960s. According to historian Donald L. Fixico, "termination essentially implied the ultimate destruction of tribal cultures and native life-styles, as withdrawal of federal services was intended to desegregate Indian communities and to integrate Indians with the rest of society."[53]

The BIA developed a program for each tribe targeted for termination. Tribes could either form a corporation for managing tribal properties, or they could sell assets and properties and distribute the proceeds among individual tribal members. If a tribe did not exercise one of these options, a temporary trustee could be named to liquidate the assets. Tribal rolls were to be updated so that all tribal members would receive fee payments and could make use of new health care facilities. Eligibility became an issue as the federal government asked, "Who is an Indian?" Questions of eligibility for per capita distribution of funds split even those tribes favoring termination, like the Quapaw people.[54]

The apex of the termination period was 1953–54; during the tenure of the Eighty-third Congress the docket was flooded with termination bills. In May, 1954, the National Congress of American Indians circulated a notice to tribes regarding Senate Joint Resolution 4 (January 7, 1953). This resolution proposed a constitutional amendment removing Indian tribes from the section designating with whom Congress could regulate commerce. The amendment "would invalidate substantially everything in the Code of Federal Regulations having specific reference to Indians. . . ."[55] The proposed amendment did not pass, but its introduction illustrates the effort Congress was willing to expend to terminate its relationship with tribes.

The responsibilities of the federal trust relationship were usually transferred to the respective states. Factionalism developed in many tribes scheduled for termination, such as with the Oregon Klamaths, where conservative full bloods resisted the perceived threat of severing federal responsibilities, while mixed-bloods supported the sale of tribal assets in anticipation of per capita distribution.

Identity issues became more visible. Youth were attracted by the material goods and by the greater number of activities that money could buy. The Klamath Reservation experienced a dramatic increase in juvenile delinquency. A plan was developed to assist Klamaths in adjusting to the white community experience.[56]

The Dine' experience demonstrates that it was not necessary for a tribe to be terminated officially for the effects of that policy to be pervasively felt. Among both Indian and non Indian the Wheeler-Howard Bill for Indian Reorganization had many vocal opponents, causing some Indian tribes to act with caution. Despite intense government lobbying among tribal members, in 1935 the Dine' voted the bill down. Sometimes increased acculturation took place as a tool to resist federal encroachment. A Navajo Tribal Council had been created in the 1920s, and though it had no traditional legitimacy, it was viewed as necessary in dealing with the federal government. Under termination policy the Dine' were classified as a Group 3 tribe, one that was never considered for termination. There was, however, a move toward reducing government involvement in reservation matters; this coincided with a growing sense of Dine' unity, facilitated by opposition to the stock reduction program of the 1930s.

The Rehabilitation Act of 1950 authorized the Navajo Council to allocate tribal funds. Unexpected mineral resource discoveries and exploitation would move the tribe toward a position of fiscal autonomy during the following decades. Political autonomy was strengthened in 1955 when local chapter governments were recognized and incorporated into the tribal government, which, along with the Tribal Council, created a two tiered representative political system.

Alabama-Coushatta personal and corporate identities were affected by termination of their relationship with the federal government in a unique way. The direct impact of federal abrogation of the trust responsibilities was minimal. The bulk of support funds was already being supplied by the state of Texas. There was no selling of land, no direct payments, and no mixed-bloods lobbying for termination and assimilation. Life and identity, however, were changing socially and politically for these reservation residents. There was movement toward more proficiency in English, and the Tribal Council, which had lain dormant for a decade, was reinvigorated and compelled to act as tribal advocate.

The Alabama-Coushatta terminated their relationship with the federal government in 1954 amid confusion about the implications of that decision. Their relationship with the federal government was unique because of the existing state involvement on the reservation. Subsequent to the 1928–30 federal and state appropriations for land purchase, education, and physical improvements, the Board for Texas State Hospitals and Special Schools continued to finance and administer various areas of reservation life.

In October, 1951, Gov. Allan Shivers suggested developing a "model Forestry Conservation project" on the reservation.[57] Andrew J. Battise, Tribal Council Chairman, notified C. H. Jones, Reservation Superintendent, in March, 1952, that the tribes desired "that you take the necessary steps in arranging with the Texas and United States Forestry Service an agreement . . . regarding the commercial cutting of timber."[58] Seventy-five percent of the proceeds were to be earmarked for buying more tribal land.

White officials were not hesitant to use intimidation to achieve their goals. On February 13, 1953, William Wade Head, Area Director of the Department of the Interior, addressed a general tribal meeting. Tribal meetings were (and still are) conducted in the Albamu language, because some in the tribe were uncomfortable speaking English. Head, speaking through a translator, began by indicating the unique relationship of the tribe with the state: "There is not another state in the Union who [sic] makes appropriations to an Indian reservation except the state of Texas."[59] He then presented a resolution upon which he wanted a vote taken that evening.

The resolution authorized the state of Texas to assume all responsibility for the "management, protection and conservation" of the tribes' forest resources. When some of the Indians hesitated at voting immediately, Head told them that Governor Shivers wanted the program initiated, and that "if they didn't vote on it[,] it would look like they just didn't care much about their affairs or their reservation."[60] Some tribal members wanted to postpone the vote until the tribal meeting scheduled for the next night, but Head told them that they had 30 percent of their voting members present (56) and that they should vote immediately.

Discussion was then held about whether a resolution could be passed without the presence of the chief: "In this kind of meeting I always thought that the Chief of the Tribe should be present? He may not have heard of this meeting."[61] Head replied, "The Constitution does not say anything about a chief. This is a democratic meeting right here, and you are practicing real democracy."[62] The several members who wanted the Chief present then left the meeting.

At this meeting Clemson Sylestine stated that this kind of issue formerly had been discussed at Tribal Council meetings. He asked if anyone could remember when the last one had been held, and no one replied.[63]

The resolution presented by Head was passed unanimously, 43–0. Termination of federal involvement in the forestry resource management was mandated and would proceed regardless of the Indians' hesitancy. The following month the Texas Senate, with the House concurring, passed a resolution that in the event of the U.S. Congress passing legislation severing its relationship with the Alabama-Coushatta, then the governor would be authorized to accept "a transfer of the trust responsibilities of the United States respecting the lands and other assets of the Alabama and Coushatta Indian Tribes. . . ."[64]

From the tribes' perspective, the sole issue was forestry. They wanted the state to develop a program on the reservation but believed that the state could be involved only if the relationship with the federal government ended. To that end, the tribes passed a resolution in June, 1953, requesting "a complete transfer of the trust responsibilities and authorities from the Federal Government to the State of Texas."[65] Prior to termination the only ongoing federal assistance provided to the reservation was funding for education, $18,000 in 1953. Texas had allocated $41,000 the same year for tribal concerns.[66]

On July 27, 1953, Rep. Ken Regan introduced House Resolution 6282, "A bill To terminate Federal trust responsibility to the Alabama and Coushatta Tribes of Indians of Texas. . . ."[67] Thirteen days later House Resolution 6547 was submitted by Representative John Dowdy. This proposed legislation would "transfer certain lands to the state of Texas to be held in trust for the Alabama and Coushatta Indians. . . ."[68]

Dowdy then visited the reservation and reported to Glenn Emmons, Commissioner of Indian Affairs, that the tribes were "greatly disturbed by this proposal." Whether because of inaccurate translation or inadequate explanation, the Indians believed that "the only thing they passed a resolution agreeing to, was that some provision might be made that the State of Texas Forest Service be permitted to supervise the operation and management of the Indian reservation lands. . . ." They were afraid of losing other benefits and "insisted that they did not intend by their resolution . . . to ask that they be deprived of their rights to go to the Indian trade schools and Indian hospitals and the many other privileges they have as Indians."[69]

In fact, termination would not affect access to Indian boarding schools, and the state assumed responsibility for health care. At the time, however, this was certainly not clear to the Indians. Dowdy believed that "the Alabama and Coushatta Tribes are probably the least ready of any Indians in the United States to be cast loose. . . . The tribes assured me that if the United States were getting out of the Indian business entirely, then they would go along and do the best they could, but they do not feel they should be selected as victims and cast adrift."[70] The federal government had successfully instilled a sense of dependency upon itself among the Indians, and the impending cessation of that relationship, however tenuous, invoked a concerned, if not fearful, response.

Two days later at a tribal meeting a resolution was passed stating that the Alabama-Coushattas had believed that they would have the opportunity to read and vote on both the Congressional proposal and on the new state charter before these were implemented. The resolution requested that Congress refrain from acting on the proposed bill until the tribal members had "an opportunity to fully understand the bill and also vote on whether or not it meets our approval."[71]

This incident suggests that the Indians were uncomfortable with the governmental proceedings yet felt compelled to acquiesce to federal mandates. When their children's health and education became an issue, however, they were willing to request that the process be halted long enough for them to come to an understanding of all the implications of the proposed actions. In spite of the paternalistic relationship, the tribe was unwilling to "simply go along" without questioning the process. They also were unwilling to allow an outside influence, the government agent, into this meeting that seemed to have so many implications for their future. C. H. Jones, Jr., the reservation superintendent, was not invited, "although I knew such a gathering was in the making."[72]

Two days later Head attended a tribal meeting on the reservation where these concerns were presented and discussed. He explained that there were no government supported Indian colleges. A resolution was passed recommending that federal funding be continued to hospitals and secondary level trade schools for five years.[73]

The following day the General Council Chairman Matthew Bullock wrote the Commissioner of Indian Affairs and made three requests:

(1) that government hospitals remain accessible for five years;

(2) that trade schools of the Indian Service be available for five years; and

(3) that tribal lands "shall never be disposed of without the approval of the majority of the adult members of the tribes."[74]

On July 1, 1955, the Interior Department announced that federal supervision of the Alabama-Coushatta Indians of Texas would end. Texas was to assume all federal obligations under Public Law 280. Little changed overtly under state auspices. Tribal Council meetings eventually resumed, and Texas established a forestry program. But other changes effected during the decade of the 1950s had long-term ramifications.

The transition in cultural identity between 1930 and 1960 included almost every area of life. When Interior Department Special Commissioner Roy Nash had visited the 250 reservation residents in 1931,[75] they spoke Albamu, Koasati, and a Mobilian trade language comprising many Choctaw words.[76] By 1960 young people spoke English to each other, and the trade language was forgotten or incorporated into Albamu.[77]

Commissioner Nash had found a central complex of buildings surrounding a square courtyard, a design easily recognizable a century earlier. What would not have been familiar was the purpose of the buildings. A new Presbyterian Church (funded by Presbyterians from around the state and built in 1930), had been erected on the former dance ground. The agent's quarters and teachers' quarters, a new hospital, the old school, and a workshop completed the complex.[78] Residential units were still primarily the old-style log cabins. Nash estimated the material wealth of a family of five in 1931 to be a log cabin, a state-erected frame cottage, a stove, two beds, four chairs, two tables, cooking utensils and clothing worth $20.00, five acres under cultivation, one plough, one horse or mule near starvation, ½ cow, six chickens, and ten pigs.[79]

In 1960 the log cabins were gone, replaced first by frame homes and later by brick units. The central complex was preparing for the advent of tourism. Agriculture and animal husbandry was replaced by off-reservation labor and tourism.

In 1930 some western medical practices had been introduced by Dr. Chambers and visiting health professionals. In 1931 Dr. W. W. Flowers reported these medical conditions on the reservation:

(1) hookworm, caused by the oversight of not building latrines for the new houses;
(2) malaria;
(3) tuberculosis;
(4) minimal venereal disease;
(5) pellagra;
(6) cardiac problems; and
(7) widespread malnutrition.[80]

While white doctors and nurses treated these medical conditions, many Indians still turned to traditional healers. In 1960, however, the medicine people's reputation had been almost completely undermined, and the reservation had a clinic with professional staff.

Public religious expressions in 1931 were exclusively Presbyterian. The Indians were even financially supporting missionary endeavors to other nonwhites in mission fields as distant as the Congo and China.[81]

In 1930 Texas Presbyterians donated funding to build a new church building. The Chambers remained until 1936, and in 1937 Oscar Landry became pastor of the Indian Village church. A bachelor, Landry was encouraged by his parishioners to marry. They believed that if he had a wife he would not make so many trips home to his family. He married in 1943.[82]

One of Oscar Landry's goals was to foster interaction with the non-Indian community. A means of facilitating this was the opening of a trading post with Presbyterian funds. The trading post, housed in a log cabin, sold baskets, beadwork, and other art and craftwork. It also served as a focal point in the tug-of-war between the two white influences on the reservation: the missionary and the government agent. The agent wanted the trading post open on Sundays, and the pastor did not. The pastor won.[83] This conflict is symbolic of the power struggle that sometimes erupted between the two cultural power brokers on the reservation.

Athletic pursuits completed the transition from Indian to white during these three decades. At the beginning of this period, stickball, or *tele*, was played on a field near Woodville, about twenty miles east of the reservation.[84] Roy Nash described the field as being 350 feet long with ten-foot-high goal posts at either end. The number of players varied, with Nash observing twenty-six.[85] In 1960 stickball had not been played for years, having been completely supplanted by basketball, softball, and volleyball.

Marriage and divorce patterns were divided in 1931 between those couples practicing the traditional example of simply moving in together and those observing Christian rites.[86] By 1960 the former pattern of polygyny was completely replaced with the more European model of serial polygamy and extramarital liaisons. According to tribal members Armando Rodriguez and Joe John, illicit relationships were seldom conducted in secrecy, with children being told which trails to avoid at certain times because lovers were meeting there.[87]

Throughout the period, non-Indian writers perpetuated the myth of "racial purity." Harriet Smither stated in her 1932 *Southwestern Historical Quarterly* article that "through all the years the Alabamas have maintained their racial integrity. . . ."[88] Avocational historian Mary Donaldson Wade wrote that "contrary to the usual practice where whites and Indians or negroes and Indians have lived in close proximity, the Alabamas have never intermarried with either of these, but have kept their racial integrity intact."[89]

This perception of absolute racial purity, however, is incorrect. There were sexual liaisons with both whites and blacks, although not extensive.[90] By 1960 Indians were experiencing wider contacts with the non-Indian community, more mixed-blood children were being born, and more marriages with non-Indians were taking place. Because clan membership was inherited through the mother, many children with non-Indian and non-Alabama-Coushatta mothers were excluded from clan participation. This situation was addressed by the creation of a "no-clan" clan.[91]

Mary Donaldson Wade stated that the children in 1936 knew little of the significance of Alabama pottery design, and many would not admit to knowing any Alabama stories or legends. This lack of cultural awareness continued to increase until the end of this period, when an intensive program to reintroduce "Indian" crafts and dances was initiated in anticipation of tourism.[92]

Despite her unmitigated praise of the missionaries, Wade suggested "that their contact with the white man has given the Alabamas a hopeless feeling," creating a "racial despondency."[93] One such site of contact was in the town of Livingston, where overt racism remained evident throughout the period. Present Tribal Administrator Jo Ann Battise remembers as a youth in the 1950s taking the weekly bus trip to Livingston on Saturdays. As the Indians descended the steps of the bus, shopkeepers would yell "the Indians are coming," and some would close their doors. One clothing store sold merchandise to the Indians but would not allow them to try on an article before purchasing it.[94]

The church attempted to deal with the repercussions of cultural genocide and racism through increased efforts at acculturation. The belief that Indian culture had been entirely eradicated is, however, misleading. Choctaw anthropology student W. E. S. Folsom-Dickerson and his family resided on the reservation for several months in 1940. His initial impression that the Alabamas and Coushattas had lost their cultural representations and completely replaced them with those of the whites was dispelled when he discovered a small group of dancers and singers sequestered in the woods late one evening. He subsequently found that many traditional cultural expressions were maintained covertly or were being reintroduced by Coushattas from Louisiana.[95] This remained the pattern on the reservation for the remainder of the twentieth century: overtly devout assimilated Presbyterians (and later Baptists and Assembly of God members, whose churches opened in the 1950s) who covertly, often unconsciously, were also traditional practitioners.

The great changes effected by the two cultural forces of church and state certainly imply victimization of the Indians. That is not to say, however, that the Alabama-Coushattas were merely pawns in a great cultural chess game. As a group and as individuals they made decisions based on the desire to survive. The most critical decision was to surrender their traditional cultural value of community and replace it with that of individual achievement and aggrandizement. As an ideology, amassing personal material resources replaced acting for the common good. This objective would become even more deeply entrenched in the following thirty years. Individual competed with individual for limited resources, and there was no annual busk to repair the ensuing personal and familial rifts.

CHAPTER 5

Ethnogenesis and Regenesis

Tribal social forms have always existed but they
have been buried during past years by the legal
entanglements of the federal government. Consequently
Indians have come to believe that their problems were
soluble by conformity to white culture (if there is one). Now
that Indian people have realized that their problems are legal
and not cultural, legal solutions will be found through
political action, and Indian people will not only be free
to revitalize old customs, but also to experiment
with new social forms.

—*Vine Deloria, Jr.,*
Standing Rock Sioux

In the mid-eighteenth century John Daniel Hammerer devised a plan to "civilize" the American Indian. For his initial endeavor he chose the Creek Nation because they were already well on their way toward becoming "civilized." He proposed to sail from England, settle in a Creek town, and instruct the inhabitants in agricultural and other practical skills. Thus they would be prepared for the Gospel and for civilization.[1]

Although there is no record of Hammerer fulfilling his aspirations, during the subsequent three centuries others accomplished his purpose. By 1960 there was little, other than the Albamu language still used by the elders, to distinguish the Alabama-Coushatta reservation community from surrounding Polk County residential enclaves. The old Indian ways had apparently all but died without so much as a last gasp.

The work of the missionaries to coerce assimilation, combined with other external forces such as reservation superintendents, television, and increased non-Indian presence on the reservation, was successful enough that adult education researcher Donald Fairweather could report in 1976 that the Indians were assimilated and shared virtually all the values of their white neighbors.[2]

During the 1960s and 1970s an extensive tourist complex was developed and generated large revenues, as did increased mineral exploitation. The tourist initiative, with its non-Indian visitors and workers, was the single greatest externally derived force of the period 1960–95.

Two new churches had also been introduced to the reservation community. A Southern Baptist church attracted primarily off-reservation Coushattas who did not feel welcome at the Presbyterian church, and an Assembly of God church, built just off the reservation in 1948, was also soon filled with Indians.[3] The process of assimilation progressed to the extent that some children were apparently unaware of their own identity. Former reservation Superintendent Walter Broemer relates that during the 1970s a young Indian boy was watching a vintage Hollywood western on television. After cheering the successes of the cowboys, he thought for a moment, looked up and said, "Someday I wish I could meet a real Indian."[4]

Subsequent to the inauguration of tourism, and consequent to it, was the introduction of supratribal activities such as powwows. These included learning the songs and dances of other tribes, donning dance regalia inspired by Plains Indians, and utilizing English as a *lingua franca* in order to communicate with other dancers. Young Alabama-Coushatta singers and dancers today know few, if any, of their own tribal songs and dances. When one young dancer was asked if he knew any Alabama-Coushatta songs, he responded by stating that he was only interested in learning powwow songs.[5] The tribes' acknowledged medicine man, Jack Battise, states that he is the only one left who remembers the old songs.[6] The single greatest concern of the elders is that the one cultural vestige not eschewed by the missionaries and others, their language, is being lost. Few young people today understand Albamu or Koasati, and even fewer will attempt to speak one of those languages.[7]

In spite of all the evidence of forfeited culture, and partially in an attempt to replace those ethnic representations, the years 1960–95 on the Alabama-Coushatta reservation witnessed a birthing process. No longer faced with the overriding need to develop and implement physical survival efforts, tribal members, both collectively and individually, began initiating cultural survival strategies. These have included both ethnogenesis, the formulation of a new ethnic identity ("Indian"), and ethnic regenesis, the reimplementation of discoverable former cultural attributes. Frequently these previously practiced cultural expressions had not disappeared but had moved underground. Those newly created cultural practices are almost exclusively supratribal in nature. The two most visible examples of this phenomenon are powwows and tourist-related activities.

The Alabama-Coushatta were not unique in experiencing these phenomena of regenesis and ethnogenesis. After World War Two Native Americans throughout the continent were in the process of reasserting their tribal identities and participating in a reawakening of what Vine Deloria, Jr. called "Indian nationalism."[8] Ethnogenesis became increasingly evident as Indians interacted with other tribes and with non-Indians. From the political arena of "Red Power" protests and Indian organizations' lobbyists in Washington, to the social realm of the powwow, Indians sought and expressed greater common bonds and expressions.

The practice of forming intertribal associations was not without precedent. Patterned after white reform associations, the Society of American Indians was established in 1911 to lobby for change in federal Indian policy. This was followed in the 1920s by the National Council of American Indians and the Oklahoma Society of Indians, and in 1934 the American Indian Federation was formed to challenge the implementation of the Indian Reorganization Act. Returning Indian veterans of World War Two were instrumental in forming the first permanent, national, political supratribal movement in 1944, the National Congress of American Indians. By 1955 fifty percent of their delegates were women, and the organization stipulated that at least one woman sit on the executive board.[9]

Other Indian political entities followed. The American Indian Chicago Conference convened in June, 1961, with 450 delegates from 90 tribes. It prepared a Declaration of Indian Purpose calling for abandonment of termination, for education access, and for reorganization of the Bureau of Indian Affairs to allow more local control in determining and applying policy.[10] All of these organizations followed the accepted practice of lobbying for changes through legislative and judicial channels. Participation in these and similar groups allowed Indians from diverse tribal backgrounds to identify common issues and goals. It also reinforced the awareness of frequently similar experiences vis-à-vis the government and the church.

The federal termination and relocation policies of the 1950s caused a dramatic influx of Indians into urban areas and fostered the creation of new social and political entities. Desiring social interaction and attempting to address common needs, many of these urban Indians began meeting and forming organizations. Adam Fortunate Eagle (Chippewa) remembers that in 1958 he "began to notice a surge of young reservation Indians brought to the Bay Area (San Francisco) under the federal program of relocation. Indians began to find each other, partially out of a sense of loneliness and confusion in their new urban surroundings and partially out of an urge to share a cultural identity."[11]

These urban Indians created in the 1960s and 1970s new groups that aggressively took their concerns to Congress, to states, to courts, and to the public. Separated from the reservation and its admittedly limited resources, they often experienced an increased sense of powerlessness. Following the example of the civil rights movement, Indian organizations abandoned petitionary protest in favor of mass action and calls for public attention.[12]

Proponents of the most visible and vigorous action came to be identified as the red power movement.[13] Adopting tactics borrowed from African-American civil rights leaders and organizations, Indians initiated three events that illustrate this phenomenon: the November, 1969, to June, 1971, takeover of Alcatraz; the 1972 Trail of Broken Treaties caravan and occupation of the Bureau of Indian Affairs building in Washington; D.C., and the 1973 Wounded

Knee standoff. In the first example, the occupiers of the defunct California federal prison suggested that the island be utilized as

(1) a "Center for Native American Studies";
(2) an "American Indian Spiritual Center";
(3) an "Indian Center of Ecology";
(4) a "Great Indian Training School" (trades, arts, and crafts); and
(5) an "American Indian Museum."[14]

The government suggested that Alcatraz be turned into a national park with an Indian theme, an offer the Indians refused.[15] Note that all of these statements use the inclusive designation of "Indian," evidence of the salience of supratribal nomenclature in political action. The occupation received national attention and support from white liberals.[16]

The latter two of these three events were conducted by the American Indian Movement, which also had members at the Alcatraz takeover. First called Concerned Indian Americans, the organization was founded in July, 1968, in Minneapolis, Minnesota. Problems with the acronym CIA encouraged a rapid name change to the American Indian Movement (AIM). At first primarily concerned with the urban Indian problems of unemployment, inadequate housing, and ineffective education, AIM soon began addressing Indian issues at the national level, which included rural and reservation concerns.[17]

In 1972 a caravan trip to Washington, D.C., called the Trail of Broken Treaties, was organized to demonstrate and publicize grievances peacefully. This plan failed upon arrival in the capital when the government provided neither the promised facilities nor the officials for negotiations. On November 2, 1972, the Indians occupied the Bureau of Indian Affairs building and barricaded the doors. Five days later the premises were vacated, BIA officials were fired, and the protesters were given $66,000 for travel expenses.[18]

The following year AIM acted again. Angry with the policies of assimilationist Lakota Tribal Council Chairman Richard Wilson, and seeking publicity for ongoing Indian issues, AIM supporters on February 27, 1973, seized the small community of Wounded Knee on the Pine Ridge Reservation in South Dakota. The Federal Bureau of Investigation sealed off the village and the confrontation received worldwide attention. Negotiations ended the standoff after seventy days, with the miserable living conditions of many Indians and their limited access to self-determination vividly driven home to American society.[19]

The experiences of these activists created strong relationships between Indians of many tribes and diverse Indian heritage. Blood quantum issues became less significant as the focus shifted to common goals and shared enemies. Michael Haney (Creek-Seminole), a participant at Wounded Knee, stated that determining Indian identity was not difficult: "If their rifle barrels were pointed at you, they weren't Indian. If they were pointed the same direction as yours, they were Indian."[20] Although the primary relationship for the Indian participants remained with the tribe, there was a growing awareness of a supratribal identity forged under fire. This was an Indian identity with little precedent, an identity created from a contemporary context. AIM became an almost surrogate tribe for some, with a shared language (English), mutual values (abstinence from drugs and alcohol), a general respect for and participation in some form of Indian-derived religious belief, and common political goals.[21]

While Indian political activists developed new relationships in an ethnogenesis rooted in common purpose, a concomitant supratribal social phenomenon was also at work in both urban and reservation settings. During the 1950s and 1960s intertribal powwows were increasingly held in gymnasiums and outdoor arenas across North America. These Native American celebrations with multigenerational participants affected perceptions of identity that were untouched by the more urban, youthful activists. A social activity with religious overtones, the modern powwow consists of dancers from diverse tribes competing for prizes in various categories, social dances open to everyone, Indian giveaways (the practice of honorees publicly giving items to the community), much visitation among families and friends, and various artisans displaying their crafts.[22]

Powwows began to proliferate in the 1950s to honor returning military veterans. According to Winnebago dancer Boye Ladd, the intertribal nature of powwows encouraged the resolution of former enmities and the creation of a new personal identity: "Back in the fifties there was still a lot of animosity between tribes. You wouldn't see Crows and Cheyennes or Crows and Sioux sitting at the same drum, let alone being at the same powwow. Today intertribalism is very much alive. The modern-day powwow has brought a lot of tribes together, it's brought unity. We are saying 'we' now as opposed to saying only 'Sioux,' 'Cheyenne,' or 'Crow.'"[23]

Most of the dance forms at a powwow derived from Plains Indian traditions that were adopted and adapted by other tribes throughout the continent. The most familiar to non-Indians is the "fancy dance," the origins of which can be traced to 1925. In that year the Haskell Institute, in Lawrence, Kansas, held a championship dance contest. The "grass dance," an Omaha tradition, was enhanced at this event by the addition of colorful feather bustles. This unique regalia and dance style was called "fancy dance" and spread throughout Indian North America.[24]

Diverse tribes adopted powwow forms of dance, and they began to conduct powwows themselves. The Alabama-Coushatta, however, learned the dances and adopted powwow regalia as part of an economic survival strategy introduced by a non-Indian. Walter Broemer arrived on the reservation in 1957 to assume the position of reservation superintendent. Concerned with the non-productive efforts at agriculture, timber, and mineral production, Broemer and the Tribal Council introduced the concept of tourism as income-producer in 1962.[25] A major component of the proposed tourist package was exhibition dancing, with the most flamboyant, and therefore the most marketable, being "fancy dance." The introduction of this dance form on the reservation with the subsequent inauguration of an annual powwow was the critical factor in the evolution of a supratribal consciousness on the Alabama-Coushatta reservation.

Earlier twentieth-century Indian dances on the reservation, both Alabama-Coushatta and other styles, were either abortive or clandestine. The first recorded instance of Plains-style Indian dances on the Alabama-Coushatta reservation was in 1936. A group of Comanches visited Houston for Texas Centennial ceremonies and stopped at the reservation on their return north to Oklahoma. A celebration, including Indian singing and dancing, was held to honor the group. Convinced by the missionaries that Indian cultural expressions were evil, many Alabamas and Coushattas chose not to attend. The Comanche leader, Baldwin Parker, son of Quanah Parker, encouraged the Texas Indians to dance their old dances: "We must not try to be a white man ourself. We must learn new things but we must keep our old way too." Several dances were held in the subsequent months, but interest quickly dissipated without the external Indian support.[26]

A University of Texas anthropology student and mixed-blood Choctaw, W. E. S. Folsom-Dickerson, spent four months living on the Alabama-Coushatta reservation in 1940. Late one night he discovered old, blind Charlie Boatman singing while a group of young people danced. They wore leggings, gorgets, and turbans, and their faces were painted. Mcconico Battise, who had acted as interpreter for the group that had gone to Washington, D.C., in 1928, explained that Charlie was married to a Coushatta woman, and they lived off the reservation.[27] The young dancers were also Coushatta, and there was widespread interest in restoring the old dances.[28] Several more were held during the following months before once again being suppressed. The next record of Indian dancing on the reservation was under the auspices of the Tribal Enterprises tourism program in the early 1960s.

When Walter Broemer came to the reservation as superintendent in 1957, he was immediately enmeshed in controversy. He replaced Howard Jones, who had attempted to pursue a primarily agricultural-oriented economy for the reservation. A rancher by profession, Jones spent his days on his ranch and, according to Broemer, made infrequent visits to the reservation in the evenings. In 1956 Chief Sylestine and Chief Battise went to the state legislature requesting greater autonomy and changes in the relationship with Jones. The legislature formed a twelve-man investigatory committee that then called for a comprehensive audit of the reservation. Subsequently, the Texas State Hospital Board, the controlling agency for the reservation, removed Jones from his position.[29]

Immediately upon his arrival Broemer called a tribal meeting to discuss problems on the reservation. The most pressing, he believed, were the absence of a functioning tribal government, the shortage of income other than insufficient state aid, and an almost complete lack of recreational opportunities.[30] Broemer soon began planning an economic package that would rely heavily on developing a viable tourist program and included limited exploration for mineral resources. Tourism, Broemer believed, would produce income for the tribe and employ tribal members.

His suggestion of introducing Indian dancing to the reservation met with strong resistance and eventually required a tribal vote before implementation. Broemer was in continual conflict with Oscar Landry, pastor of the Presbyterian Church from 1937–52 and 1956–71,[31] and other church members over the issue of tourism. There were two petitions to remove Broemer from his position, but his supporters on the reservation prevented his expulsion.[32]

One area of identity that was dramatically altered by the introduction of tourism was the role of chief (mikko). From the point at which the missionaries first arrived, authority vested in traditional figures was eroded. For almost a century, however, the chief retained the ultimate political and social decision-making role. With the inauguration of the tourist industry, this changed.

In 1936 Bronson Cooper Sylestine and Robert Fulton Battise were installed as mikko choba and mikko atokla (first and second chiefs) at a much-publicized ceremony. They took an active leadership role in church, society, and politics. As illustrated earlier, it was considered inappropriate for decisions affecting the tribe to be considered without their presence. By the time of his death in February, 1969,[33] Chief Cooper Sylestine's role had altered considerably. He perceived that he had become a mere figurehead, a symbol of Indianness.[34] He greeted visitors to the complex in headdress and regalia and acted as goodwill ambassador at official functions. Broemer attributes some of the chief's discomfort to Oscar Landry, the Presbyterian missionary, who continued to seethe over the reservation complex being opened on Sunday, Indians wearing pre-Christian regalia, and "heathen" dancing. Broemer claims that Landry manipulated the chief through Cora, the chief's daughter, and exacerbated divisions in the tribe regarding tourism.[35]

Landry's efforts, combined with Chief Sylestine's uncomfortable transition of role and perceived loss of power, increased factional friction with Broemer. On October 18, 1968, a meeting was held in which another petition for his removal, bearing sixty-nine names, was discussed by tribal members and the Texas Commission for Indian Affairs. Cora Sylestine, the chief's daughter and spokesperson, expressed concern that Broemer was violating traditional Alabama-Coushatta procedural protocol and was forcing expansion of tourism too rapidly. The commissioners rejected the request, and Broemer remained.[36] The superintendent further alienated his opponents by attempting to obtain personal statements of loyalty from tribal employees, a significant blunder, according to his own account.[37]

Support for Broemer by many Indians was perceived by Chief Sylestine to be evidence of further erosion of his authority, which caused him great disappointment. Contradictory to tribal precedent, his funeral was private, with entrance by invitation only. He stated before his death that the tribe had not supported him in life and need not be present at the services following his death.[38] Robert Fulton Battise was inaugurated as mikko choba and Emmett Battise as mikko atokla on January 1, 1970.[39]

The Tribal Enterprise Tourist Project was initiated in 1962, and within ten years the reservation budget grew from $72,039, all state-appropriated funds, to $344,014, of which only $75,662 was provided by the state. Twenty full-time and eighty part-time Indian employees catered to the wishes of over 100,000 visitors in 1967.[40] The tourist endeavor continued to expand throughout the following decade. In 1969 an Economic Development Grant provided the tribe $209,000 for further development of the tourist complex,[41] and in 1971 state and federal assistance totaled over $1,000,000.[42] A dam and campground were constructed, creating a thirty-acre lake and visitor recreational complex. A new restaurant, dance arena, and council house were added to the tourist complex.[43]

Tourism subsided in the late 1970s because of the general downturn in the economy.[44] Today it is not a profit-producing activity, but it does provide many jobs for reservation residents.[45] The greatest impact of the introduction of tourism on the reservation was increased Indian self-esteem through the implementation of powwow style dancing and annual powwow ceremonies. It also signaled a period of growing supratribal activity.

There were charges from within and outside the reservation of inappropriately profiting from being Indian, to which Byron

Price, Presbyterian minister from 1972–85,[46] replied, "sure they're commercializing their heritage. . . . These people are selling what they know. They're trying to make a living."[47]

In 1963 Frank Marcos, a Pueblo Indian from Taos, was brought to the reservation through federal funds secured from the Area Redevelopment Agency. He came to teach "hoop" dancing and other "fancy" dances. Jack Battise subsequently formed the Na-ski-la (Dogwood) Dancers in 1963 to provide exhibition dances for the reservation's tourists and for other local events such as the "Forestry Festivals."[48] He and his "powwow committee" also coordinated the first powwow on the reservation. Held the evening of July 19, 1969, the event was open to visiting Indians and to the general public.[49] This became the first in an uninterrupted series of annual powwows. There was a recognition that ethnogenesis was taking place: reporter Stephen Harrigan noted in 1975 that the chiefs' regalia had been "lost and reinvented."[50] Another re-porter, Herman Kelly, suggested that the Indians were "fighting to perpetuate their ethnic culture," and that even though the dances are "no longer Comanche, Apache, or Pawnee . . . they are Indian, and that's all that matters."[51]

This invention of a new, supratribal identity continued as more vestiges of Alabama-Coushatta culture were replaced by outside-derived representations. Deni Sylestine, a champion dancer, estab-lished the Alabama-Coushatta Indian Club in 1979 to foster and celebrate Indian heritage. It began as an Indian dance organiza-tion, but evolved into a social club that sponsors a biennial dinner to honor Indian veterans, takes trips to important Indian sites, and assists with powwows. Deni remembers when visiting Indi-ans complemented the female dancers on their traditional Ala-bama-Coushatta regalia. During the last five years, she says, the Alabama-Coushatta women have all adopted powwow dresses from other tribes. She believes that the progressive loss of Alabama-Coushatta culture was due to a lack of courage by tribal leaders in responding to the cultural onslaught of the church.[52]

One impact of the increased supratribal awareness in the so-cial setting was similar to that of the Indian political activists. Young people involved in powwows learned from other tribal youth that they shared many similar experiences with the government and the church. This heightened recognition of a common historical experience and the role of outside cultural forces was expressed in 1971 by eighth-grader Nita Battise: "Today many Indians have become members of Christian churches, but find it hard to appreciate the teachings of Jesus when they meet so little brotherly love in the white men who profess this gospel."[53] Two decades earlier it would not have been acceptable for a student to display publicly such a sentiment.

A generation after the introduction of annual powwows, many youth embrace these dances as part of their own culture. Bryan Williams, championship dancer, explains that "families teach their children the traditional (powwow) dances at an early age. It's a way to learn about your heritage and show pride in your own people."[54] A century earlier Williams's reference to other tribes' dances and heritage as his own would not have been possible. The supratribal context of powwows made that statement accurate, given the transformed nature of Indian identity.

Concomitant with increased participation in supratribal activities was the increasing perception that being Indian was acceptable in the context of white society. The success of Tribal Enterprises tourist activities and the large non-Indian attendance at the annual powwows (often numbering several thousand)[55] demonstrated widespread interest in Indian cultural expressions. The resulting increased confidence in the value of Indian identity and concern over economic survival, translated into political activity in the 1980s, as the tribe sought to reestablish its relationship with the federal government. This process, however, began two decades earlier.

The Texas State Board of Hospitals was reorganized in 1965, but the Indians were not included in the new agency.[56] Legislation was introduced and passed that created the Texas Commission on Indian Affairs. No director was appointed, and Walter Broemer was named to fill the position temporarily. In January, 1972, Broemer left the reservation to assume full-time control of the Texas Indian Commission.[57]

By the 1980s Alabama-Coushatta relations with the state were becoming strained. The tribe continued to expand facilities and services, necessitating requests for additional state funding at a time when Texas purse strings were tightening.[58] Although restoration of the federal relationship could have great economic implications, it was a 1981 dispute over three deer that acted as a catalyst for the process of regaining federal recognition. A question of hunting jurisdiction and licensing arose, and Texas Attorney General Jim Maddox issued an opinion that no Indian reservation existed in Texas.[59]

The state legislature seized this opportunity and cut all funding to the reservation. A federal judge overruled the state attorney general, but negotiations had already begun with the Bureau of Indian Affairs for reinstatement of a trust relationship with the federal government. On August 18, 1987, the five-year process of restoration was completed and federal recognition restored.[60] Not willing to let its identity as American Indian, nor its existence, be questioned, the tribe challenged the state. This increased propensity to challenge non-Indian authorities is indicative of the continuing ethnic transformation. Unwilling to chafe in silence, they found a voice for their frustrations. This voice is increasingly being heard as older cultural expressions are being revived.

An underlying current of traditional Alabama and Coushatta ethnic memory has survived intact among some of the elders, although it is frequently silent and has not generally been passed on to the more assimilated youth. Rarely evident in the past to the non-Indian observer, this rich tribal resource is moving toward a more visible and active status. A vivid example of this ethnic regenesis, as contrasted with ethnogenesis, is the Alabama-Coushatta federal hair case.

In August, 1992, three teenaged boys—Danny John, Gilman Abbey, and Emanuel Williams—were told that they could not register at Big Sandy High School until they cut their hair to the length designated by the school dress code. All three of the young men participated in powwows as singers and dancers, and they were intent on maintaining the long hair of their Alabama-Coushatta ancestors. Initially, they spoke with several Cherokee mixed-blood friends, stating that every year administrators forced them to cut their hair, but this year they wanted to fight the school on this requirement. The friends suggested that the youth discuss the issue with their parents and with tribal leaders, which they did.[61]

Within a few days these boys and two elementary school students who also refused to cut their hair were allowed to register but were immediately placed in "in-school suspension." The parents met with the author to determine an appropriate course of action. They believed that the Tribal Council would not support their efforts, but they were wrong. Tribal Council Vice-Chairman Roland Poncho spearheaded the effort to support the young men.

Several weeks later a large group of adults from the reservation, including Tribal Administrator Jo Ann Battise, attended a Big Sandy School Board meeting and requested that Indian boys be exempted from the mandated hair length. After a brief discussion the board voted against the request. The Tribal Council retained an attorney, Donald Juneau, to pursue the case. He filed in federal district court on behalf of the tribe and twelve students,[62] and after several months a temporary restraining order was issued allowing the boys to return to class.[63]

Juneau planned a presentation based on the principle of religious freedom. The preliminary injunction hearing was heard by Fifth Circuit Court Judge William Justice in Tyler, Texas, on January 4, 1993. Juneau called anthropologist Hiram Gregory, who stated that long hair was traditionally worn by the Alabamas and Coushattas. Tribal Administrator Jo Ann Battise and the boys testified, relating long hair to their "sincerely-held religious belief." The school's attorney questioned the boys regarding their participation in church. He stated that if they were Christians, then maintaining long hair could not be a "sincerely held religious belief." Danny John, who at one time indicated that he would like to pursue a legal degree, listened carefully to the school's lawyer's words and noted the direction he was leading the witnesses. When on the stand, Danny was asked if his father, Joe John, had been an Assembly of God minister, and Danny answered "yes." Then Danny was asked if he was a Christian. He thought for a moment, and responded, "I used to be."[64]

The deeply emotional nature of Indian identity was demonstrated by one of the witnesses called by the school's attorney, an Indian woman who worked for the school. While on the stand, she began weeping and stated that the Indian children referred to her as an "apple" (red on the outside and white on the inside).[65]

The nature of Alabama-Coushatta identity and the forms of its cultural expression can be as emotional an issue as the identity of urban mixed-blood Native Americans.

Testimony took no more than several hours, with little in the way of cultural background being presented. The transition in cultural identity was manifest in statements showing that while parents who were practicing Christians and who did not believe long hair to be spiritually relevant, nevertheless completely supported their children's beliefs and encouraged them to respect tribal customs and traditions.[66]

Judge Justice, unhappy with the brevity of prepared testimony by the tribe's attorney, angrily told Juneau that he had set aside three days from a busy schedule to hear the case and had expected to be informed thoroughly about the culture of the Alabama-Coushattas. Juneau was told that he had two months to prepare adequate written testimony before a ruling would be made.[67]

Juneau subsequently contacted Native American historians, including Vine Deloria, Jr., who provided information that was ultimately included in Juneau's brief. Justice ruled in favor of the Indian boys, and Big Sandy appealed the decision. Juneau stated that when the case was heard in the Fifth Circuit Court of Appeals in New Orleans, one of the Justices stated that it was ridiculous for the school to be concerned with hair length when other schools were dealing with guns and knives in the classroom. The two sides were instructed to attempt to negotiate a resolution before a ruling was handed down.[68] Big Sandy subsequently "adopted a new, more punitive regulation, requiring a notarized application and hiding the hair in the shirt-collar."[69] The tribe protested, and the new regulations were curtailed.

Another indication of ethnic regenesis is the creation of the Cultural Preservation Committee. There is a fear among many on the reservation that this generation of elders will be gone soon, and that with their passing they will take the bulk of the Alabama-Coushatta cultural knowledge. Of special concern is the potential complete loss of language within the next generation. Children continued to learn English at earlier ages through Headstart and kindergarten programs. By the mid-1970s one generation after the reservation school closed, young people were speaking English as their first language.[70]

A related concern is that young people know little of the history and status of other Indian nations. A group met on the reservation several times in May and June, 1995, to address these issues. The group comprised Jack Battise (an elder), Armando Rodriguez (the tribal storyteller), Rochellda Sylestine (14), Ezekiel Rodriguez (14), Michelle Battise (18), and Frank Polite (15). Zetha Battise subsequently joined the group. The current Presbyterian minister, Dr. Pamela Morgan, suggested that the group apply for funding from the Self-Development Program of the Presbyterian Church. A grant proposal for $5,000 was written, submitted, and approved.

The name of the project, *Istayokpa,* means "to honor." Their proposal states that much of the despair suffered by Indian youth today is a result of having their culture forcibly removed. In an attempt to begin to address the situation, the group suggested two areas of activity. One is to travel to other reservations to learn about other Indian nations, and the other is to have young people document their elders telling tribal stories, teaching craftwork, and reciting their own experiences. During the trip to other reservations the youth would camp and listen to an accompanying elder relate Alabama-Coushatta tribal history.[71] Grant funds enabled the purchase of two video cameras and related equipment and camping equipment.

The group traveled to Pine Ridge Reservation (South Dakota) and Little Big Horn Memorial (Montana) during the first week of July. After visiting the Wounded Knee site, they camped in the badlands immediately north of the reservation. There, while sitting around a campfire, Jack Battise discussed their language with them, and encouraged Rochellda Sylestine, the young person most fluent in Albamu, to continue using her linguistic skills. Jack then produced a cassette tape, and the small group of Alabama-Coushattas began dancing in the flickering firelight to the stomp dance music, their own traditional dance.[72]

Two months after returning from this trip the group met again at a home near the reservation. This time a *tele* pole and goal were set up and lacrosse sticks obtained. The young people played for several hours, then set up their tents and built a fire. After supper the stomp tapes were produced and people danced. Later, Zetha Battise and Jack Battise related stories about the reservation. Subsequently, the group's equipment was also used to video tape a tribal display of artifacts, with narration in English and Albamu.[73]

Efforts at ethnogenesis and regenesis continue at an increased pace, although not without resistance. Church influence is pervasive, and Western values are still highly venerated. The externally introduced cultural force of tourism led to the development of a local dance group and subsequently, to powwows. This conscious ethnogenesis of a new "Indian" cultural identity was successful because it captured the imagination of both the Alabama-Coushattas and the surrounding non-Indian communities, despite resistance from the church. The new confidence engendered by this phenomenon produced a more visible display of specifically Alabama-Coushatta cultural expressions, such as pine-needle and river cane basketwork and beadwork. Some tribal members are today exploring the possibilities of reintroducing formerly held cultural practices like stomp dances and stickball games. Perhaps most significantly, church members are questioning the all-encompassing forfeiture of their ancestors' cultural expression to the demands of the church.

Conclusion

*Historical contrast if too blankly presented may obliterate
the subtler forms of change and survival. . . . Contrast
over time, furthermore, might conceivably be allowed
to divert attention from contrast over space, or rather
cross-cultural comparison. . . .*

—*Peter Laslett,
Historian*

The purpose of this project was to illustrate the dynamic and contextually based nature of personal and communal ethnic identity. The Alabama-Coushatta Indians of East Texas provided the case study. As their culture changed in response to external cultural forces, so, too, did their personal identities. Although these tribes were spared the violence experienced by most other Indian nations, the cultural loss was dramatic. The benevolent paternalism of church and state devastated Alabama-Coushatta cultural identity during the late nineteenth and early twentieth centuries. Ironically, that same government paternalism, through efforts at economic revitalization, fostered the phenomenon of ethnogenesis in the second half of this century.

The concomitant regenesis of Alabama-Coushatta ethnic practices indicates both the volition and environment necessary for cultural continuity. Physical survival is not the critical issue it once was (and still is on many reservations, such as Pine Ridge and Rosebud in South Dakota). This context allows a cultural adaptation and flexibility that is particularly evident in the subtler ethnic expressions.

Alabama-Coushatta cultural transition during the past five centuries has been extensive. As with all cultures, their ethnic change over time included the mutation of existing expressions and, frequently, the replacement of indigenous manifestations with externally derived forms. Transition resulting from a response to internal forces may best be described as cultural modification. This type of ethnic change is visible in western society in language, religion, attire, art forms, and the like. English, German, French, and Spanish remain the means of communication in England, Germany, France, and Spain, and all are in a constant state of mutation. Christianity, with its diverse sects, is still the dominant religion. A logical progression is evident in western music, painting, sculpture, and literature. Even clothing maintains threads of continuity. Modification of cultural expressions may appear diverse and unrelated while sharing a common origin.

Native American society also exhibits modification of traditional forms. More evident, however, is the replacement of Indian cultural expressions with those derived from the external forces of western European origin. Many Indian communities experienced this type of transition in virtually every facet of life, including religion, language, community ideology, economy, gender roles, family structure, and diet. Because communal and personal identities are mutually interdependent, the imposition and adoption of these cultural artifacts caused a corresponding transition in personal identity. Conversely, as a majority of individuals altered their ethnic expressions, communal identity respectively changed. When the group's identity mutated, those shared expectations determined for succeeding generations, to a significant extent, their perceptions of personal identity. Alabama-Coushatta society experienced both modification and replacement of cultural expressions, which led to a significant transition in personal identity.

Areas in which modification of existing forms are evident include political expressions, gender roles and social relationships, language, layout of residential households in the greater community context, and religious practices and beliefs. Traditional political structures comprised the nonhereditary mikko and advisory councils, whose leadership roles were divided between periods of military activity and peace (red and white). The position of mikko exists today, although in an essentially symbolic capacity. The Tribal Council is composed of elected representatives, including women, and is the supreme decision-making body on the reservation. Within the larger geopolitical framework, the relationship of the Alabamas and Coushattas to the Creek confederacy was more elective than is the ward-guardian relationship with the Texas and U.S. governments.

Social relationships were modified, although not as dramatically as might be expected. Polygyny is not legal, but premarital and extramarital liaisons are common, as is serial polygamy. Cohabitation and parenthood frequently precede state-sanctioned marriages, and children often reside for long periods with grandparents.

Women retain significant roles as tribal leaders, as illustrated by those currently serving in the positions of tribal administrator, Indian Health Service head nurse, and two seats on the Tribal Council. One was nominated for chief, and she was included on the ballot in the last election. Women are also frequently clan elders, thus exercising authority as critical components of a traditional system that has been retained in a very limited form. The exclusionary nature of matrilineal clans was addressed in the last decade through the introduction of a "No-clan" clan, for those whose genetic connection to the Alabama-Coushatta comes from the father rather than through the mother.

Linguistic expression was modified early in this century when English was introduced and incorporated in church and school. Albamu, Koasati, English borrowings, and the Mobilian trade language combined into what is today identified as Albamu or "Indian." Excepting the English-derived vocabulary, these were never written languages. English is now the dominant language among young people and may soon completely replace "Indian."

Residential habitation patterns have also been modified. Early non-Indian attempts to determine an estimate of Alabama-Coushatta population were hindered by the Indians' traditional community layout. Widely dispersed households were loosely grouped around a town where political, religious, and economic activities were conducted. These homesteads were frequently undercounted by early census takers. Today, the same pattern exists. Roads meander through the reservation, with homes spaced at least several hundred yards apart, hidden in the Piney Woods.

Religious belief and expression have also been significantly modified. A substantial case could be made positing that Christianity supplanted rather than modified traditional beliefs, and that this cultural transformation would be better allocated to the replacement category. The role of religion in Alabama-Coushatta life, however, remains similar to that of the past. Deity is perceived to be beneficent. Spiritual purification is necessary and available. Public gatherings on a regular basis are necessary for spiritual health. There is an afterlife. These components are common to both Christianity and traditional belief. Remnants of former religious ideology remain in numerous areas of cultural expression, including the prevalence of belief in the efficacy of Indian "medicine" (occult manipulation of people and environment), the presence of spirits and other supernatural creatures, and the funerary practice of placing personal possessions of the deceased on the grave.

Although modification of cultural forms has been extensive, equally as significant to contemporary Alabama-Coushatta identity is the replacement of one indigenous cultural expression or ideology with another derived from an external source. In the case of the Alabama-Coushatta, these cultural replacements include town layout, athletic participation, and economy. The most critical and pervasive cultural replacement is in the ideology of individual vis-à-vis community.

Layout of the central buildings in the community is new, and the former administrative, commercial, athletic, and religious areas of communal activity are gone. The council house was replaced with an administration building, the dance arena with a Presbyterian Church, and the stickball and chunkey field with a gymnasium (for basketball and volleyball). Dispersed throughout an area adjacent to the tourist complex, these structures no longer form a complex with the arena in the center. Other common-use areas such as the community center, health clinic, daycare facility, and softball field are located about a mile away from the central complex.

An agricultural economy was replaced with one dependant on government resources, mineral exploitation, tourism, and individual on- and off-reservation employment. Communal economic activities such as hunting, gathering, and harvesting were supplanted with individual-oriented employment. Even those employed by the tribe in various endeavors, including tourism, administration, forestry, security, and health care, are monitored for individual presence and achievement. That most Western of cultural artifacts, the time clock with punch cards, is endemic at reservation offices.

The ascendancy of the western-derived role of the individual is the single greatest change in Alabama-Coushatta culture, with ramifications in virtually every cultural area. Primary allegiance is to the economic well-being of the individual and immediate family, rather than to the community. Religious salvation is through personal faith and practice instead of through communal rites and participation. Contrary to former values, personal material wealth is pursued and is particularly evident in the many new vehicles, televisions, and home furnishings.

The loss of a community-oriented ideology is pervasive and continues to erode. Tribal Administrator Jo Ann Battise remembers how her family used to go visiting every Sunday afternoon. Today, however, "when people see you driving up, they close the door."[1] The social support networks that were formerly in place, such as extended family, clan, and community, have been supplanted by the western institutions of church and state, which have proven inadequate in dealing with contemporary problems.

The replacing of a community welfare ideology with one of self-interest impedes decision making by tribal leaders. They themselves may be willing to sacrifice for tribal benefit, but they cannot be assured that anyone will join them in their efforts. Health issues such as pervasive alcoholism and fear of a growing HIV/AIDS presence remain essentially unaddressed. Ostensibly, education is strongly encouraged. Students are, however, increasingly dropping out of high school, and those going on to college find themselves ill-prepared. Parents provide little motivation and discipline for educational excellence. In practice, the adopted western ideology has primarily produced despair.

For a century young people have been encouraged to "become white" in order to survive. This necessitated forfeiting the old cultural expressions and Native American identity, which they did. Today reservation youth have neither traditional Alabama-Coushatta mechanisms for moral and emotional success nor adequate support from white institutions of church, school, and government. Given the deteriorating state of both Indian and white cultural agencies, it is not surprising that some reservation youth are asking, "What will become of this reservation in the future?"[2] The answer to the question of cultural survival lies in regenesis.

Alabama-Coushatta ethnic regenesis is not erupting *ex nihilo*. Although obscured from off-reservation observers, many elements of tradition continue to be quietly practiced by some elders and a few youth. Indian medicine is utilized. Personal items are placed on graves for the continuing journey. Spirits and "the little people" walk, usually unseen, on the land.

There was a brisk early afternoon breeze that was somewhat blocked by the tarps hanging across the east side of a recently constructed arbor. Jack Battise had just finished using his eagle feather fan and tobacco in blessing the small center arena where baby Norris Lee Littlestar Seward would have his four-month haircut. Parents, grandparents, and friends listened intently as Armando Rodriguez explained that this child, who represented the future, must learn about his past. Armando's brother, Roland, agreed to be Norris's mentor in teaching him what it means to be Indian. The boy, himself a mixed-blood and truly symbolic of today's Alabama-Coushatta, also has an adopted white grandmother.

Roland and the other singers at the drum rendered a song composed for the occasion. It then became the property of the child, and any other singer must obtain his permission before singing it. The ceremony was followed by a giveaway and barbecue dinner.[3]

This young child inherits a five-hundred-year legacy of cultural transition instigated by Columbus's arrival in this hemisphere. External cultural forces imposed on Alabama-Coushatta society have elicited survival responses that transformed their culture. Beginning with the early impact of Spanish-borne diseases and continuing with missionary and government influence, life was continually, dramatically altered. Most Native Americans share(d) a cyclical perception of time and space. Therefore, it is fitting that after the past century of cultural divestment and transformation, Alabama-Coushatta youth of today are expressing increased interest in their own cultural past.

Other reservations have experienced similar phenomena. Lucille Silk has been a mental health care professional at the White Earth Reservation Indian Health Service clinic in Minnesota for twenty-two years. An Ojibwa tribal member, she believes that loss of Indian identity and traditional practices has significantly contributed to the alcoholism that is endemic in the Native American community. Federal imposition of identity guidelines was also destructive to mental health. Prior to the 1960s the tribe designated its members through community ascription. People of all degrees of Indian blood who resided and identified with the tribe were fully accepted. Then, under federal pressure to limit liabilities, a 1/4 minimum blood quantum was imposed for future enrollees.

Today, Silk encourages the reassertion of Indian identity and the return to traditional language and practices as a key to mental health.[4] Some Alabama-Coushattas also believe that it is time for a reimplementation of former beliefs. In June, 1995, a group of teenagers from the Alabama-Coushatta reservation attended a large conference in San Diego, California. Sponsored by the United Native Indian Tribal Youth (UNITY) organization, over one thousand Indian young people from across the country participated. The single greatest issue with which the youth were concerned was that of substance abuse. From reservations everywhere came story after story about the destructiveness of alcohol and its effects on Indian people. Two factors were apparent on reservations where the battle against alcohol and despair was being won: a concerted direct effort by the tribal government and the reimplementation of traditional tribal values and practices—ethnic regenesis.[5] Alabama-Coushatta youth participated in the various meetings, then commented that they wanted to see the situation change on the reservation, but it seemed to them that no adult would listen.[6]

The problems faced by reservation communities in successfully addressing alcohol abuse and despair are indicative of an inadequate response to external cultural forces. According to Lucille Silk, alcohol abuse is a problem that resulted from contact with whites. Addressing it at a community level requires strong direct leadership. It is ironic that Alabama-Coushatta have survived in part because of their overtly pacific nature. Tribal leader Roland Poncho explained that the Alabama-Coushatta Indian "never confronts a situation directly."[7] This indirect approach to conflict resolution worked well for thousands of years in precontact Indian society during which the entire community functioned under the same cultural paradigm. It has also been successful for much of recent Alabama-Coushatta history because of their pacifistic and insular relationship with non-Indian society. The Alabama-Coushattas have never needed to sign a treaty with a European or with the U.S. government. This cultural style is not, however, an adequate method for addressing contemporary externally imposed issues, especially since such a large proportion of supporting elements of traditional culture was surrendered. There is, for example, no mechanism in place today similar to the traditional busk, where individuals, families, and clans agreed to forgive transgressions, reconcile, and begin anew.

For many tribes, culture brokers have been utilized to assist in devising strategies for surviving externally derived threats.[8] The Alabama-Coushatta currently have no successful culture broker whom they trust to aid in dealing with current problems. Consequently, externally imposed threats such as alcoholism and HIV, combined with a traditional nondirect style of leadership, pose some of the tribe's greatest challenges to cultural survival.

The means of achieving continued ethnic survival is learning to "walk in both worlds." Those threats that are externally imposed must be dealt with directly, while at the same time a more traditional community-oriented ideology must be established. Individuals and Indian communities that have reasserted ties to culturally specific tribal beliefs while incorporating western-style methods in addressing non-Indian-derived issues have proven successful. Both cultural worlds must be studied, understood, and navigated.

As with any people, the hope for the future of the Alabama-Coushattas is in their children. Pride must be instilled in them as individuals and in their heritage as Indians and as Alabama-Coushattas. The latent racism of focusing on blood quantum issues needs to be addressed, particularly as more youth choose non-Indian spouses and sexual partners. When older people speak with pride about being "full-blooded" Indian, what does that do for the self-esteem of their mixed-blood children and grandchildren? Blood quantum has been substituted for culture, skin color substituted for tradition, individual substituted for community.

Tomorrow's promise of continued successful Alabama-Coushatta cultural existence lies in further regenesis of tradition and ethnogenesis of Indian identity, directed by a strong leadership. These, however, cannot be imposed by outside forces. Paternalism and coercion are equally powerful tools in cultural genocide. Many well-intentioned non-Indian and Indian culture brokers believed that they knew what was best for the Alabama-Coushattas and how to achieve these goals. Frequently they have been surprised and indignant when tribal members and leaders did not immediately and enthusiastically endorse their plans. The initiative for positive change must come from within the tribe itself.

Culture is dynamic, and transition is inevitable. As our culture changes, so does our individual identity. Alabama-Coushatta identity is determined by many factors: Alabama-Coushatta tradition, Christian expectations, federal and state definitions, white stereotypes, and personal perceptions. Each of these is dynamic, and every individual filters these ethnic forces through his or her own unique experience. It is impossible to define Indian identity outside of a specific context, because to do so would make static that which is dynamic. An accepted definition of "Indian" in one spatial-chronological context is inadequate or inappropriate in another. It is, however, useful to evaluate specific cases of ethnic transition, such as the Alabama-Coushatta, in order to understand how ethnic identity is created and recreated. Volition plays a large role in cultural transformation, within environmental parameters, and we consciously choose to employ both positive and negative cultural expressions. As we understand the process better, we may decide to inculcate an esteem for those cultural artifacts that contribute to a more healthy future.

Jack Battise looked around at the light blue Wyoming sky. There were a few small clouds floating very high and very far away above the plain. He had just finished a short, joyful dance of gratitude. Tangled sagebrush nagged at his feet as he climbed, but he had made it to the top. Uh-li-la-mo-lo, thank you, Abba Mikko, Grandfather

Creator. Stooping to take a handful of the wet snow, he watched Jordan, the young boy of Cherokee descent, run barefoot through the mud and ice. Almost sixty years ago, when he was about this boy's age, he had learned some dances from a group of visiting Comanches. He thought about how important those and other dances had become to him, how he had seen the powwows continue to grow, and how the children today had never known a time without Indian dances. Now, if they could just learn their own traditional stomp dance.

Several hundred yards away three Alabama-Coushatta teenagers played in another small patch of wet July snow. Two of them chased each other around, trying to drop melting snow down the other's collar. Then Frank and Michelle stopped and held hands, and Jack remembered his first crush. It was during the same Comanche visit when he saw the most beautiful girl in the world. Quanah Parker's teenaged granddaughter's feet seemed to float as she danced in her white buckskin dress. Although he was only eight, she captured his heart.

There had been many changes in his and the tribe's life since then, and Jack wondered what the future held for this young couple. He saw Rochellda toss a snowball at them to disrupt their romantic reverie, and he said a prayer of thanks for her. She cared about being Alabama-Coushatta, about the language and about the traditions. One of the few reservation youth who enjoyed speaking Albamu, she was also successful in school and a leader at church. She knew that she was Indian, was Alabama-Coushatta, and she was proud. As long as youth like Rochellda continued to speak the language and practice the old traditions, what there was left of them, the people would survive.

Jack thought back to earlier in the week, as he stood by the mass grave at Wounded Knee. Indians had lost much, had endured much. Then he remembered the two eagles he saw earlier that day, remembered that the Creator continued to care for and protect them. The circle was not broken, and he smiled.

Notes

Chapter 1. Ethnicity and the American Indian

1. The term "identity" is itself ambiguous. For an analysis of this multifaceted concept see Thomas K. Fitzgerald, *Metaphors of Identity: A Culture-Communication Dialogue*. For the purposes of this paper, identity is defined as the perception of self-in-context.

    "Culture" also has many definitions. In this work the definition of El Colegio de Mexico Professor Rodolfo Stavenhagen will be used: ". . . the broad spectrum of human activities, symbols, values, and artifacts that identify a human group and distinguish it from others." Rodolfo Stavenhagen, *The Ethnic Question: Conflict, Development, and Human Rights*, p. 2.

2. Karl EschBach, "Shifting Boundaries: Regional Variations in Patterns of Identification as American Indian," Chapter 7, unpublished manuscript, 1992, p. 1.

3. American Indian Lawyer Training Program, Inc., *Indian Tribes as Sovereign Governments: A Sourcebook On Federal-Tribal History, Law, and Policy*, p. 34.

4. "All members of the Cherokee Nation must be citizens as proven by reference to the Dawes Commission Rolls. . . ." *Constitution of the Cherokee Nation of Oklahoma*, Article III, Membership, Section One, p. 4, ratified June 26, 1976. The General Allotment Act (Dawes Act) rolls officially closed in 1906.

    An Alabama-Coushatta baby will be automatically accorded tribal membership "provided both parents are of all Indian blood" (Article II—Membership, Section 1, paragraph b). Mixed-blood Alabama-Coushattas and Indians from other tribes married to Alabama-Coushattas may be adopted by submitting a formal request to the Tribal Council. The "decisions of the Tribal Council shall be subject to popular vote at the next election." *Constitution and By laws of the Alabama-Coushatta Tribes of Texas,* Article II—Membership, Section Six.

5. Ted Robert Gurr, *Minorities at Risk: A Global View of Ethnopolitical Conflicts,* p. 3.

6. Thomas Hylland Eriksen, *Ethnicity and Nationalism: Anthropological Perspectives,* p. 4.

7. John Milton Yinger, *Ethnicity: Source of Strength? Source of Conflict?* p. 3.

8. "The members of the corporation shall be individual Native Americans, of one-quarter Indian blood, 18 years of age or older, and must reside within the Houston Metropolitan area." *By-Laws of the Inter-Tribal Council of Houston,* 1978, Article II—Membership, Section One.

9. Deborah Scott, President of Cherokee Cultural Society of Houston, personal interview.

10. Lorilee Lipke, Executive Director of the American Indian Chamber of Commerce, Houston, personal interview.

11. Wilma Mankiller, former Principal Chief of the Cherokee Nation of Oklahoma, personal interview.

12. Chad Smith, Cherokee Nation of Oklahoma tribal attorney and 1995 candidate for Cherokee Principal Chief, oral presentation to Cherokee Cultural Society of Houston, March, 1995.

13. Russell Thornton, *American Indian Holocaust and Survival: A Population History Since 1492,* pp. 188–89.

14. Armando Rodriguez, Alabama-Coushatta tribe member, personal interview.

15. Yolanda Poncho, Alabama-Coushatta Tribal Registrar, personal interview.

16. Terry P. Wilson, "Blood Quantum: Native American Mixed Bloods," in Maria P. P. Root, ed., *Racially Mixed People in America,* p. 109.

17. For an account of the Lumbee situation, see Karen I. Blu, *The Lumbee Problem: The making of an American Indian people.*

18. For a recent account of the Texas Cherokee experience, see Dianna Everett, *The Texas Cherokees: A People Between Two Fires, 1819–1840.*

19. Charles Boudreaux, Cherokee, personal interview.

20. Gary B. Nash, *Red, White and Black: The Peoples of Early America,* p. 246.

21. William T. Hagan, "Quanah Parker," in R. David Edmunds, ed., *American Indian Leaders: Studies in Diversity,* p. 181.

22. Larry P. Aitken and Edwin W. Haller, *Two Cultures Meet: Pathways For American Indians to Medicine,* p. 93.

23. Charlotte Johnson Frisbie, *Kinaalda: A Study of the Navajo Girl's Puberty Ceremony,* pp. 384–86.

24. Ibid., p. 387.

25. For an account of alcohol consumption among the Navajo, see Stephen J. Kunitz and Jerrold E. Levy, *Drinking Careers: A Twenty-five-year Study of Three Navajo Populations.*

26. Anastasia M. Shkilnyk, *A Poison Stronger Than Love: The Destruction of an Ojibwa Community,* p. 16.

27. For an analysis of the dynamic nature of ethnicity see Pierre L. van den Berghe, *The Ethnic Phenomenon.*

28. The most poignant succinct account of the Ghost Dance and the events at Wounded Knee, although written by a non-Indian, remains Dee Brown, *Bury My Heart at Wounded Knee: An Indian History of the American West,* pp. 415–45.

29. George De Vos and Lola Romanucci-Ross, eds., *Ethnic Identity: Cultural Continuities and Change,* p. 176.

30. The term "western" is used exclusively in this work to denote culture derived from western European antecedents, and should not be misinterpreted as referring to the "Old West" of the United States.

31. Charles Boudreaux, personal interview.

32. Eugeen E. Roosens, *Creating Ethnicity: The Process of Ethnogenesis,* pp. 46–47.

33. Ibid., p. 98.

34. Vine Deloria, Jr., *Custer Died for Your Sins: An Indian Manifesto,* p. 265.

35. For an account of attempts to form intertribal associations during the seventeenth and early eighteenth centuries, see Gregory Evans Dowd, *A Spirited Resistance: The North American Indian Struggle for Unity, 1745–1815.*

36. Stephen E. Cornell, *The Return of the Native: American Indian Political Resurgence,* p. 107.

37. Ibid., p. 141.

38. The author was a participant in the meetings to determine appropriate survey questions and criteria for interviewee inclusion. He personally interviewed thirty people for the survey.

39. Joane Nagel, "Constructing Culture," *American Indian Ethnic Renewal: Red Power and the Resurgence of Identity and Culture,* p. 10.

40. Deborah Scott, Charter Board Member, Native American Methodist Church of Houston, personal interview.

41. Jack Battise, Alabama-Coushatta elder and former Chairman of the Alabama-Coushatta Powwow Association, personal interview.

42. Cherokee "traditional" powwow and "stomp" dancer, Ed Ketcher, personal interview.

43. "Indian Days" Coushatta Celebration Program.

44. 1994 Cherokee National Holiday Program.

45. One early challenge to the "melting pot" theory was Nathan Glazer and Daniel Patrick Moynihan, *Beyond the Melting Pot.*

46. For an analysis of the resurgence of ethnic diversity among whites, see Richard D. Alba, *Ethnic Identity: The Transformation of White America.*

47. Richard H. Thompson, *Theories of Ethnicity: A Critical Appraisal,* p. 11.

48. Only one of over one hundred American Indians surveyed by the author did not believe in some form of genetically transmitted cultural memory.

49. N. Scott Momaday, "Personal Reflections," in Calvin Martin, ed., *The American Indian and the Problem of History,* p. 158.

50. Mary Crow Dog and Richard Erdoes, *Lakota Woman,* p. 92.

51. Malcolm Chapman, "Social and Biological Aspects of Ethnicity," in Malcolm Chapman, ed., *Social and Biological Aspects of Ethnicity,* p. 21.

52. Composite drawn from multiple interviews.

Chapter 2. Early Contact
to Reservation Establishment

1. Black Elk, *Black Elk Speaks: Being the Life Story of a Holy Man of the Oglala Sioux, as told through John G. Neihardt,* pp. 194–95.

    The circle is most eloquently depicted in ceremonial dance. In the clockwise movement of the Plains groups and the counterclockwise circle of the Cherokee and other eastern nations, the circle is alive and balance is maintained. Cherokee Principal Chief Wilma Mankiller comments on the role of the dance and eschatology: "There is an old Cherokee prophecy which instructs us that as long as the Cherokees continue traditional dances, the world will remain as it is, but when the dances stop, the world will come to an end. Everyone should hope that the Cherokees will continue to dance." Wilma Mankiller and Michael Wallis, *Mankiller: A Chief and Her People,* p. 29.

2. Lame Deer/John Fire and Richard Erdoes, *Lame Deer: Seeker of Visions,* pp. 112–13.

3. Calvin Martin, "The Metaphysics of Writing Indian-White History," in Calvin Martin, ed., *The American Indian and the Problem of History,* p. 8.

4. "Except for what we read in books, we just don't know our own history." Alabama-Coushatta tribal member, Joe John, personal interview.

5. Howard N. Martin, *Myths and Folktales of the Alabama-Coushatta Indians of Texas,* p. 3; John R. Swanton, *Early History of the Creek Indians,* Bureau of American Ethnology, Bulletin 73, p. 192.

6. Swanton, *Early History of the Creek Indians,* p. 191.

7. Henry F. Dobyns, *Their Number Become Thinned: Native American Population Dynamics in Eastern North America,* p. 11.

8. Ibid., p. 343.

9. Russell Thornton, *American Indian Holocaust and Survival: A Population History Since 1492,* pp. 32 and 42.

10. Cabeza De Vaca, *Adventures in the Unknown Interior of America,* translated and annotated by Cyclone Covey with a new epilogue by William T. Pilkington, pp. 85–89.

11. Dobyns, *Their Number Become Thinned,* pp. 263–64.

12. Ibid., pp. 15–21.

13. James Adair, *The History of the American Indians,* p. 259.

14. Jack Battise, personal interview.

15. Edward Gaylord Bourne, ed., *Narratives of the Career of Hernando de*

Soto in the Conquest of Florida, as told by a Knight of Elvas and in a relation by Luys Hernandez de Biedma, Factor of the Expedition, also based on the Diary of Rodrigo Ranjel, his Private Secretary, Ranjel section, pp. 109–11.

16. Ibid., Biedma section, pp 24–25. See also R. B. Cunninghame Graham, *Hernando de Soto, Together with an Account of One of His Captains, Goncalo Silvestre,* p. 164.

17. Bourne, *Narratives of the Career,* in Elvas section, p. 108.

18. Swanton, *Early History of the Creek Indians,* p. 193.

19. Daniel Jacobson, "Written Ethnological Report and Statement of Testimony: The Alabama-Coushatta Indians of Texas and the Coushatta Indians of Louisiana," in *Alabama-Coushatta (Creek) Indians,* p. 37.

20. Swanton, *Early History of the Creek Indians,* pp. 193–96.

21. For a concise summary of southeast Indian resistance to British encroachment, see Nash, *Red, White, and Black,* pp. 132–40.

22. From 1718 through 1734 Antoine Simon Le Page du Pratz lived in Louisiana, and he resided half that period with the Natchez Indians. In his *History* du Pratz places the Alabama nation on the Mobile River just above the bay and says that "they love the French, and receive the English rather out of necessity than friendship."

23. Bossu, *Travels In The Interior Of North America, 1751–1762,* p. 130.

24. William Bartram, *The Travels of William Bartram,* p. 294.

25. Major C. Swan, United States Army, in Henry B. Schoolcraft, *History, Condition and Prospects of the Indian Tribes of the United States: Collected and Prepared Under the Direction of the Bureau of Indian Affairs, Department of the Interior,* pp. 264–66.

26. Bartram, *The Travels of William Bartram,* p. 284.

27. Bossu, *Travels In The Interior Of North America, 1751–1762,* p. 142.

28. One consequence of contact with Europeans was the reduction of visible political power for Indian women. Europeans assumed that female leadership was either temporary or auxiliary, that they were merely appendages of their husbands. Alice Beck Kehoe, *North American Indians: A Comprehensive Account,* pp. 192–193.

29. Fred B. Kniffen, et al. *The Historic Indian Tribes of Louisiana,* p. 164.

30. Swan, in Schoolcraft, *History, Conditions and Prospects,* p. 265.

31. Bartram, *The Travels of William Bartram,* p. 251.

32. Bossu, *Travels in the Interior of North America, 1751–1762,* p. 144.

33. Ibid., p. 152.

34. Adair, *History,* p. 150. Vestiges of the law of retribution are still extant in tribal memory. Dorcas Bullock, Nita (Bear) clan elder and sister of Chief Robert Fulton Battise, relates the following story which she first heard as a young girl from her father:

> *One day a man went hunting. Ahead of him he saw two rattlesnakes sitting in the road. As he started to go around them, one called to him: "Come Here! We want to talk with you." The man obeyed*

and came closer. "We are very sad. A girl killed our young son, and then threw his body away. She did not even bury him properly by hanging him over the branch of a tree. We want you to take our young cousin over there (indicating a short rattlesnake) to where the young girl lives."

The man agreed to do what they asked. Taking the snake to the town where the young girl lived, he placed it on a shelf in her house which was about head high. Indians love to dance, and soon everyone, including the young girl, was dancing all around, in and out of the houses. As she passed the shelf with the snake, it struck her and she died. The man removed the snake, so the people did not know who killed the girl.

The man returned to where the two rattlesnakes were sitting. They thanked him for doing as they had asked. Then they gave him a powerful gift which caused him to be successful whenever he went hunting.

Several years later the man went back to the same place to look for the rattlesnakes. He found them at the same spot, and they had grown much larger. The snakes informed him that since he had helped them to kill the little girl, he would not be allowed to go to heaven, but must remain on the earth.

Dorcas Bullock, personal interview. The epilogue with Faustian undercurrents may have been added after contact with Christians.

35. Adair, *History,* p. 150.
36. Ibid., p. 158.
37. Bossu, *Travels in the Interior of North America, 1751–1762,* p. 131.
38. Ibid., pp. 146–47.
39. Kniffen, *The Historic Indian Tribes,* p. 144.
40. Bossu, *Travels in the Interior of North America, 1751–1762,* p. 147.
41. Jean-Bernard Bossu's note in Bossu, *Travels in the Interior of North America, 1751–1762,* p. 131.
42. Kniffen, *The Historic Indian Tribes,* p. 244.
43. Bossu, *Travels in the Interior of North America, 1751–1762,* p. 132.
44. Ibid., pp. 132–33.
45. Adair, *History,* pp. 142–43.
46. Bossu, *Travels in the Interior of North America, 1751–1762,* p. 145.
47. Kniffen, *The Historic Indian Tribes,* pp. 246–48.
48. Some young widows vigorously pursued this option: "The warm-constitutioned young widows keep their eyes so intent on this mild beneficient law, that they frequently treat their elder brothers-in-law with spiritous liquors till they intoxicate them, and thereby decoy them to make free, and so put themselves out of the reach of that mortifying law. If they are disappointed, as it sometimes happens, they fall on the men,

calling them *Hoobuk Wakse*, or *Skoobale*, *Hasse kroopba*, 'Eunuchus praeputio detecto, et pene brevi;' the most degrading of epithets." Adair, *History*, pp. 189–90.

49. Kniffen, *The Historic Indian Tribes*, pp. 223–26.

50. John R. Swanton, "Social Organization and Social Usages of the Indians of the Creek Confederacy," *Forty-Second Annual Report of the Bureau of American Ethnology, 1924–1925*, p. 79.

51. Adair, *History*, p. 32.

52. Jacobson, in *Alabama-Coushatta (Creek) Indians*, pp. 47–49.

53. Christopher Vecsey, *Imagine Ourselves Richly: Mythic Narratives of North American Indians*, p. 218.

54. Bossu, *Travels in the Interior of North America, 1751–1762*, pp. 141–42.

55. W. B. Hodgson, et al., *Creek Indian History*, quoted in Jacobson, *Alabama-Coushatta (Creek) Indians*, p. 49.

56. The green corn ceremony and ritual consumption of the black-drink were the most important expressions of Creek, and therefore of Alabama and Coushatta, religious practice.

57. Vecsey, *Imagine Ourselves Richly*, pp. 219–21.

58. The Coushatta had another "harvest festival" for their mulberry crop: "These Koosahte Indians annually sanctify the mulberries by a public oblation, before which they are not to be eaten; which, they say, is according to their ancient law." Adair, *History*, p. 267.

59. The French were excellent propagandists. Adair relates how French priests taught the Indians that God had sent his son to place the Indians in a position of power over all the other inhabitants of the continent. However, as he was about to set sail from London, he was intercepted by the English and was murdered. Adair, *History*, p. 153.

60. "There existed a class of homosexuals, or berdaches, who performed the menial tasks of women. No stigma was attached to their position, and they were looked upon as 'social women.'" Homosexuality was not considered a crime and therefore was not punished. Kniffen, *The Historic Indian Tribes*, p. 244, p. 219.

61. John R. Swanton, *Myths of the Southeastern Indians*, Bureau of American Ethnology Bulletin 88, pp. 119–20.

62. Kniffen, *The Historic Indian Tribes*, p. 84.

63. Howard N. Martin, "Polk County Indians: Alabamas, Coushattas, Pakana Muskogees," *East Texas Historical Journal* 1979) 17 (No. 1, 1979): 4.

64. Jacobson, in *Alabama-Coushatta (Creek) Indians*, p. 56.

65. Herbert Eugene Bolton, ed. and trans., *Athanase De Mezieres and the Louisiana-Texas Frontier: 1768–1780*, 2:19.

66. Jacobson, in *Alabama-Coushatta (Creek) Indians*, pp. 57–58.

67. Ibid., pp. 58–59.

68. Dan L. Flores, ed., *Jefferson & Southwestern Exploration: The Freeman & Custis Accounts of the Red River Expedition of 1806*, pp. 249–50.

69. Jacobson, in *Alabama-Coushatta (Creek) Indians,* p. 62.

70. Annie Heloise Abel, ed., *A Report from Natchitoches in 1807 by Dr. John Sibley,* pp. 12–15, 19–20, 30–39, 46–47, 67–68, 82–83.

71. Dan L. Flores, "The Red River Branch of the Alabama-Coushatta Indians," *Southern Studies* 16 (Spring, 1977): 66.

72. Martin, "Polk County Indians," p. 5. Indians other than the displaced Creek contingents were also moving into Spanish and Mexican Texas. Cherokees, who had begun westward explorations in the second half of the eighteenth century to pursue game, soon began migrating in that direction. Sibley reported Cherokees on the Red River in 1807, and in 1810 several prominent chiefs and their followers migrated west, swelling the western Cherokee numbers to over 2000. Everett, *The Texas Cherokees,* pp. 10–23.

73. Virginia H. Taylor, ed., *The Letters of Antonio Martinez: Last Spanish Governor of Texas, 1817–1822,* p. 124.

74. Taylor, *The Letters of Antonio Martinez,* p. 47.

75. Dorman H. Winfrey, ed., *Texas Indian Papers, 1825–1843,* pp. 2–3.

76. Martin, "Polk County Indians," p. 5.

77. Ibid., p. 7.

78. Francis E. Abernethy, ed., *Tales From the Big Thicket,* pp. 55–57.

79. Winfrey, ed., *Texas Indian Papers, 1825–1843,* pp. 14–17.

80. Mirabeau B. Lamar, "Letter from M. B. Lamar to Colluta," July 9, 1839, and Mirabeau B. Lamar, "Proclamation from Mirabeau B. Lamar to the Citizens of Liberty County," July 9, 1839, in Winfrey, ed., *Texas Indian Papers, 1825–1843,* pp. 72–74. In his proclamation to the Liberty County citizens Lamar described his Indian policy:

> *It is the settled policy and determination of the Government to remove beyond our territorial limits every Indian tribe that has no rightful claim to reside in Texas, and such is the state of our present Indian relations, that there exists a strong hope of our being able to do this without delay, or blood shed, provided they are not exasperated to hostilities by indiscreet acts on the part of our citizens. When the emigrant tribes shall have been removed, the few which claim the right to remain will not have the means of giving us annoyance, and should they attempt it there will be no difficulty in punishing them as they deserve, but it will be impossible to carry out the policy which has been adopted for the attainment of this most desirable end, if our own people, regardless of the dictates of prudence, shall upon every slight aggression make war upon such of the scattering tribes as shall be within their reach at the moment of excitement.*

81. Everett, *The Texas Cherokees,* pp. 114–15.

82. Holland Coffee, "Affidavit of Holland Coffee," May 6, 1842, in Winfrey, ed., *Texas Indian Papers, 1825–1843,* p. 127.

83. "An Act Authorizing the President to have Surveyed a Reserve of Land

for the Coshattee and Alabama Indians," Approved 25th January, 1840, in H. P. N. Gammel, ed., *The Laws of Texas, 1822–1897,* 2:371–72.

84. Joseph L. Ellis, "Letter from Joseph L. Ellis to Thomas G. Western," in Winfrey, ed., *Texas Indian Papers, 1844–1845,* pp. 146–47. Ellis was the agent appointed to the Alabama-Coushattas.

85. Martin, "Polk County Indians," p. 8.

86. For an account of early federal Indian policy in Texas, see Robert A. Trennert, Jr., *Alternative to Extinction: Federal Indian Policy and the Beginnings of the Reservation System, 1846–51,* pp. 61–93.

87. "An Act for the Relief of the Alabama Indians," approved February 3, 1854, in Gammel, ed., *Laws of Texas,* 3:68–69.

88. Jean Louis Berlandier, *The Indians of Texas in 1830,* edited and introduced by John C. Ewers, p. 48.

89. Berlandier describes some Coushattas: "The Conchates do not look like a native people. To see them you would say they were a gathering of settlers. . . . They have chosen fertile land. They are successful farmers and sell much of their produce. They raise sheep, build houses of logs, and differ in practically no respect from the American settlers. They live at peace with everyone. Ibid., p. 124.

90. Ibid., plate 11.

91. Ibid.

92. Berlandier states that not only are watermelons grown, but a "first fruits" ceremony is held for the watermelon crop. Ibid., p. 95.

93. Torrey and Brothers, "Account of Indian Bureau with Torrey and Brothers," January 12, 1845, in Winfrey, ed., *Texas Indian Papers, 1844–1845,* pp. 165–66.

94. Educator Zetha Battise and Tribal Administrator Jo Ann Battise, personal interviews.

95. Armando Rodriguez, Alabama-Coushatta tribe member, personal interview.

Chapter 3. "Fields White Unto Harvest"

1. H. R. Runnels, "Appointment of James Barclay as Indian Agent in Polk and Tyler Counties," May 12, 1858, in Dorman H. Winfrey, ed., *Texas Indian Papers, 1946–1859,* p. 284.

2. H. R. Runnels, "Letter from H. R. Runnels to J. Barclay," June 2, 1858, ibid., pp. 287–89.

3. H. R. Runnels, "Letter from H. R. Runnels to J. Barclay," July 7, 1858, ibid., pp. 292–94.

4. H. R. Runnels, "Letter from H. R. Runnels to J. Barclay," August 20, 1858, ibid., p. 295.

5. H. R. Runnels, "Proclamation by H. R. Runnels," January 10, 1859, ibid., pp. 312–13. See also George Klios, "Our People Could Not Distinguish One Tribe from Another: The 1859 Expulsion of the Reserve Indians

from Texas," *Southwestern Historical Quarterly* 98 (Fall, 1994): pp. 598–619.

6. H. R. Runnels, "Letter from H. R. Runnels to J. Barclay," in Winfrey, ed., *Texas Indian Papers, 1846–1859*, February 19, 1859, ibid., pp. 315–16.

7. H. C. Pedigo for Antone, Cilistine, Thompson, and John Scott, "Letter from Chiefs of the Alabama Indians to Sam Houston," December 29, 1859, in Dorman H. Winfrey and James M. Day, eds., *The Indian Papers of Texas and the Southwest, 1825–1916*, pp. 389–90.

8. The undated "Polk County Historical Sketchbook" identifies these Alabama-Coushattas as members of Bullock's Company: John Abbie, Ike Battise, John Galloway, Jesse George, Jim Henderson, John Jasshet, John Johnson, Sam Kibbe, Johnson Poncho, Tom Poncho, John Scott, Alex Sylestine, Bob Thompson, Ben Walker, Sampson Williams, and six others whose names are not known. It should be noted that long-term Chief John Scott is among the veterans. Also, all of these men have European names.

9. Martin, "Polk County Indians," p. 12.

10. Ruth Peebles, *There Never Were Such Men Before: The Civil War Soldiers and Veterans of Polk County, Texas, 1861–1865*, pp. 599–600.

11. Throckmorton to U.S. Indian Commissioner, September 20, 1866, in Winfrey, ed., *Texas Indian Papers*, pp. 110–12.

12. William E. Unrau, "Lewis Vital Bogy (1866–67)," in Robert M. Kvasnicka and Herman J. Viola, eds., *The Commissioners of Indian Affairs, 1824–1977*, pp. 109–14.

13. Ibid., pp. 115–22.

14. Ibid., pp. 125–26.

15. Martin, "Polk County Indians," p. 13.

16. Jere Franco, "The Alabama-Coushatta and their Texas Friends," *East Texas Historical Journal* 27 (No. 1, 1989): 40.

17. Martin, "Polk County Indians," pp. 16–17.

18. U.S., Congress, House, "Report of William Loker and Letters to the Indian Department Relative to the Alabama Indians of Texas," July 6, 1912, 62 Cong. 2 Sess., No. 866, p. 4.

19. U.S., Congress, House, Report, *Purchase of Land, Livestock, and Agricultural Equipment for Alabama and Coushatta Indians, Texas*, 70 Cong., 1 Sess., March 2, 1928, No. 824, p. 2.

20. U.S., Congress, *An act making appropriations for the current and contingent expenses of the Bureau of Indian Affairs, for fulfilling treaty stipulations with various Indian tribes, and for other purposes, for the fiscal year ending June thirtieth, nineteen hundred and nineteen*, 65 Congress, 2 sess., 1918, 40 Stat. L. 586, Sec. 22.

21. Deni Sylestine, co-founder of the reservation Indian Club, personal interview. This organization works to promote Indian culture and to honor Alabama-Coushatta veterans.

22. C.W. Chambers, quoted in Harriet Smither, "The Alabama Indians of

Texas," *Southwestern Historical Quarterly* 36 (Oct., 1932): 107; Senate Journal, 41 Legislature, Reg. Sess., 760, 762.

23. William E. Merrem, "Merrem Tells About His Experiences, An Oral History Interview," *Texas Forestry* 24 (Sept., 1983): 7–8.

24. "The Indians in Polk County, Texas," *Dallas News,* in *Frontier Times,* Vol. 5, No. 1, October 1927, pp 30–31.

25. Clem Fain, Jr. "East Texas," *Polk County Enterprise,* April 1928.

26. U.S., Congress, *An act making appropriations to supply deficiencies in certain appropriations for the fiscal year ending June 30, 1928, and prior fiscal years, to provide supplemental appropriations for the fiscal years ending June 30, 1928, and June 30, 1929, and for other purposes,* 70th Congress, 45 Stat. L. 883-900, 1st session, 1928.

27. Texas, Senate, Special Committee Report, 41st Legislature, Regular session, 1929, pp. 760–65.

28. Mary Donaldson Wade, *The Alabama Indians of East Texas,* p. 20.

29. Henry Warner Bowden, *American Indians and Christian Missions: Studies in Cultural Conflict,* p. 167.

30. Robert F. Berkhofer, Jr., *Salvation and the Savage: An Analysis of Protestant Missions and American Indian Response, 1787–1862,* p. 6.

31. Bruce Kinney, *Frontier Missionary Problems: Their Character and Solution,* p. 82.

32. Rev. Issac T. Whittmore, "The Pima Indians, their manners and customs," in Mrs. C. W. Martin, ed., *Among the Pimas, or, The Mission to the Pima and Maricopa Indians,* pp. 93–94.

33. Charles H. Cook, unpublished sermon manuscript, October 16, 1898, p. 18. See also Minnie A. Cook, *Apostle to the Pima Indians: The Story of Charles H. Cook, The First Missionary to the Pimas.*

34. Beverly Hungry Wolf, quoted in Rayna Green, *Women in American Indian Society,* p. 94.

35. Kvasnicka, *The Commissioners,* pp. 33–34.

36. For an account of Grant's Peace Policy see Robert H. Keller, Jr., *American Protestantism and United States Indian Policy, 1869–82.*

37. Berkhofer, *Salvation and the Savage,* p. 69.

38. William G. McLoughlin, *The Cherokees and Christianity, 1794–1870: Essays on Acculturation and Cultural Persistence,* p. 16.

39. For an analysis of missionary curricula and motives see Michael C. Coleman, *Presbyterian Missionary Attitudes toward American Indians, 1837–1893.*

40. Mankiller and Wallis, *Mankiller,* p. 80.

41. Martin, "Polk County Indians," p. 16.

42. Merrem, "Merrem Tells About His Experiences," p. 8.

43. Jimmy Johnson and Jack Battise, personal interviews.

44. Ludie Battise, personal interview.

45. Dedie Williams, personal interview.

46. Delores Poncho, personal interview.

47. Clem Sylestine, et al., "The Alabama Coushatti Indian Presbyterian Church," essay, p. 5.

48. Mrs. R. S. Nettie McClamroch, "History of the Alabama Indian Church," essay, p. 9.

49. Sylestine, et al., "The Alabama Coushatti Indian Church," p. 4.

50. McClamroch, "History of the Alabama Indian Church," pp. 4–5.

51. Sylestine, et al., "The Alabama Coushatti Indian Church," p. 4.

52. Emma R. Haynes, "The History of Polk County," unpublished essay, 1937, p. 158.

53. Sylestine, et al., "The Alabama Coushatti Indian Church," p. 5.

54. McClamroch, "History of the Alabama Indian Church," p. 8.

55. Sylestine, et al., "The Alabama Coushatti Indian Church," pp. 5–6.

56. Haynes, "The History of Polk County," p. 158.

57. Walter Broemer, personal interview, September 23, 1995.

58. McClamroch, "History of the Alabama Indian Church," pp. 8–9.

59. Sylestine, et al., "The Alabama Coushatti Indian Church," pp. 6–7.

60. McClamroch, "History of the Alabama Indian Church," p. 7.

61. Deloria, *Custer Died for Your Sins*, p. 102.

62. Joe John, personal interview.

63. McClamroch, "History of the Alabama Indian Church," p. 5.

64. Zetha Battise, personal interview.

65. Wilma Mankiller, personal interview.

66. Deloria, *Custer Died for Your Sins*, p. 102.

67. McClamroch, "History of the Alabama Indian Church," p. 4.

68. I. A. Coston, "Only Indian Reservation in Texas," in *Frontier Times* 24 (April, 1947): 386.

69. Calvin Martin, *Keepers of the Game: Indian-Animal Relationships and the Fur Trade*, pp 49–56.

70. McClamroch, "History of the Alabama Indian Church," p. 5.

71. Jack Battise, personal interview.

72. Lawrine Low Battise, personal interview.

73. Joe John, personal interview.

74. Coston, "Only Indian Reservation in Texas," p. 388.

75. "Friendly Indians of the Trinity River," anonymous, *Texas Almanac, 1861,* (mistakenly listed as 1860), in *Frontier Times* 2 (June, 1925): 7.

76. Walter Broemer, personal interview.

77. Sylestine, et al., "The Alabama Coushatti Indian Church," p. 5.

78. Deloria, *Custer Died for Your Sins*, p. 105.

79. Delores Poncho, personal interview.

80. Jack Battise, personal interview.

81. Emily Sylestine, "Predicament of Alabama Indians Told by Native Girl," from the *Houston Post-Dispatch,* in *Frontier Times* 9 (April, 1932): 302. Emily's name is misspelled in the publication as Sylvestine.

82. These witches could shape-shift into other creatures, frequently dogs. They were also cruel. Dedie's uncle was a young man when the govern-

ment built frame houses in 1930. He and some friends went to one of the new houses and decided to play a joke on the man inside, who some claimed was a witch. Several of the boys took a log, inserted it under one end of the house, and levered the house up. The man was inside singing and did not hear them until their prank was achieved. When he rushed out, all of the boys fled except Dedie's uncle and a friend. The man blamed them for the incident, and soon after this her uncle became ill and died. Some blamed the witch. Dedie Williams, personal interview.

83. "Friendly Indians of the Trinity River," pp. 5–6.

84. Sylestine, "Predicament of Alabama Indians," p. 302.

85. Jack Battise, interview.

86. "Friendly Indians of the Trinity River," p. 6.

87. Ibid., p. 5.

88. Frederick Law Olmstead, *A Journey Through Texas: Or, a Saddle-Trip on the Southwestern Frontier,* p. 401.

89. "Friendly Indians of the Trinity River," p. 7.

90. Anonymous, "Tucson Training School," in *Home Missions Monthly,* November 1893, photocopy, no page number.

91. Sylestine, et al., "The Alabama Coushatti Indian Church," p. 8.

92. F. J. Hart, "Papagoes," *Presbyterian Home Missionary* 14 (February 1885): p. 35 (photocopy).

93. Wade, "The Alabama Indians of East Texas," p. 7.

94. Roy Nash, "The Indians of Texas," March, 1931, unpublished Report of the Special Commissioner, p. 21. Sam Houston Regional Library and Research Center, Liberty, Texas.

95. Berkhofer, *Salvation and the Savage,* pp. 33–34.

96. Mrs. C. W. Chambers, personal interview in Willie Ford King, "The Educational Growth of the Alabama and Coushatta Indians of East Texas," p. 18.

97. Eula Battise, personal interview.

98. Jimmy Johnson, personal interview.

99. Jack Battise, personal interview; observation of artifacts.

100. Dedie Williams, personal interview.

101. Frances Battise, personal interview.

102. Esther Battise, personal interview.

103. Ibid.

104. Dedie Williams, personal interview.

105. Mrs. C. W. Chambers, "Head Teacher or Principal's Term Report based on Teacher's Daily Register to the Superintendent of Public Schools, 1922–1923," Sam Houston Regional Library and Research Center, Liberty, Texas.

106. J. P. Galloway, "Head Teacher or Principal's Term Report Based on Teacher's Daily Register to the Superintendent of Public Schools, 1931–1932," Sam Houston Regional Library and Research Center, Liberty, Texas.

107. J. P. Galloway, "Head Teacher or Principal's Term Report based on Teacher's Daily Register to the Superintendent of Public Schools, 1933–1934," Sam Houston Regional Library and Research Center Liberty, Texas.
108. James W. Markham, "Alabama-Coushatta Indian Reservation" in *The Handbook of Texas,* 1:19.
109. Sylestine, "Predicament of Alabama Indians," p. 302.
110. Herman H. Fitzgerald, Principal, Indian Village School, "Application for Equalization Aid, 1940–1941," Sam Houston Regional Library and Research Center, Liberty, Texas.
111. Jimmy Johnson, personal interview.
112. C. H. Cook, "Pima Indians," *Presbyterian Home Missions,* 11 (August, 1882): 187 (photocopy).
113. Lawrine Low Battise, personal interview.
114. Jimmy Johnson, personal interview.
115. Ibid.
116. Zetha Battise, Esther Battise, Melvin Battise, Jimmy Johnson, personal interviews.
117. Esther Battise, personal interview.
118. Zetha Battise and Jack Battise, personal interviews.
119. "Lo, The Poor Alabamas!" *East Texas Optimist* (Woodville, Texas) October 30, 1930, derived from the *Beaumont Enterprise,* undated article, p. 2.
120. Jack Battise, personal interview.
121. Zetha Battise, personal interview.
122. Esther Battise, personal interview.
123. Dedie Williams, personal interview.
124. Although spirits are generally feared, not all are malevolent. Dedie Williams tells of one case where a spirit resided in a house. Many tenants were frightened away when it made its presence known. One day an African-American woman rented the house, but, because of her strong faith, she was not afraid of the spirit. When it appeared to her, it told her that it had been trying to give the other occupants something when they vacated the premises. The spirit instructed the woman to look under the front porch, which she did. There she found a large sum of money. She reported her find to her landlord, who told the woman that whatever she found was hers to keep. She used the money to put her children through college.
125. Jack Battise, personal interview. "Swept yards" were not an exclusively Indian practice and were evident throughout the region.
126. Ludie Battise, personal interview.
127. Lawrine Low Battise, personal interview.
128. Jack Battise, personal interview.
129. Berkhofer, *Salvation and the Savage,* p. 62.
130. Alabama-Coushatta Presbyterian Church Session minutes, August 24, 1910, pp. 9–10.
131. Merrem, "Merrem Tells About His Experiences," p. 8.

132. Lawrine Low Battise, personal interview.

133. Haynes, "The History of Polk County," p. 158.

134. Frances Densmore, "The Alabama Indians and Their Music" in J. Frank Dobie, ed., *Straight Texas: Publications of the Texas Folk-Lore Society*, p. 275.

135. Aline Roth, "Missionaries to Alabama-Coushattas Brought Light to Sun Kee's Dark Cloud," *The Houston Chronicle*, photocopy, day and month unlisted, 1946.

Chapter 4. Three Decades of Government Paternalism, 1930–60

1. Nash, "The Indians of Texas," p. 27.

2. The most prevalent dance expression to be retained by southeastern tribes, including the Cherokee, Creek, Seminole, and Choctaw, has come to be known as a "stomp" dance. The earliest description of this dance that can be logically attributed to the Alabamas or Coushattas was by Solomon Northup, a free Black in the north who was captured and enslaved in 1841, taken to Louisiana, and finally freed in 1853. In his autobiography he describes a group of Indians from Texas coming to the Louisiana Piney Woods for a "carnival" with a local Indian community. Their second chief was named John Baltese (Battise?). He states that they "worshipped the Great Spirit, loved whiskey, and were happy." (p. 72.)

His description of the ensuing dance sounds very similar (except for the "sort of Indian fiddle) to a modern "stomp" dance conducted by Creeks, Cherokees, Choctaws, or Seminoles. The only intact tribes of southeastern cultural derivation in East Texas at that time were the Alabamas and Coushattas, the Cherokees having been expelled two years earlier. It is therefore likely that the dancers observed by Northup were from one of these groups:

> When they had formed a ring, men and squaws alternately, a sort of Indian fiddle set up an indescribable tune. It was a continuous, melancholy kind of wavy sound, with the slightest possible variation. At the first note, if indeed there was more than one note in the whole tune, they circled around, trotting after each other, and giving utterance to a gutteral, sing-song noise, equally as non-descript as the music of the fiddle. At the end of the third circuit, they would stop suddenly, whoop as if their lungs would crack, then break from the ring, forming in couples, man and squaw, each jumping backwards as far as possible from the other, then forwards—which graceful feat having been twice or thrice accomplished, they would form in a ring, and go trotting round again.

Solomon Northup, *Twelve Years A Slave*, Edited by Sue Eakin and Joseph Logsdon, pp. 72–73.

3. Sylestine, et al., "The Alabama Coushatti Indian Church," pp. 9–10.

4. Joe John, personal interview.

5. Ibid.

6. For an analysis of the debate in the Continental Congress over the relationship with Indian nations, see Francis Paul Prucha, *The Great Father: The United States Government and the American Indians*, pp. 35–50.

7. U. S. Constitution, Article I, Sect. 8, Clause 3.

8. Francis Paul Prucha, *American Indian Policy in the Formative Years: The Indian Trade and Intercourse Acts, 1790–1834*, p. 2.

9. Prucha, *The Great Father*, p. 211.

10. *Worcester v. Georgia*, 31 U.S. (6 Pet.) 515, 8 L.Ed. 483 (U.S. Sup. Ct. 1832).

11. Robert A. Trennert, Jr., "William Medill (1845–49)," in Kvasnicka and Viola, eds., *The Commissioners of Indian Affairs*, pp. 33–34.

12. Prucha, *The Great Father*, pp. 317–18.

13. Paternalistic in design, the intent of the Severalty Act was to provide individual Indian families with the land and motivation to become self-sufficient. The law was frequently abused by whites who coerced or tricked the Indian owners into selling or relinquishing their lands.

14. Christine Bolt, *American Indian Policy and American Reform*, p. 99.

15. Lake Mohonk Conference Proceedings, 1885, p. 43, quoted in D.S. Otis, *The Dawes Act and the Allotment of Indian Lands*, pp. 10–11.

16. Vine Deloria, Jr., ed., *American Indian Policy in the Twentieth Century*, pp. 247–48.

17. Ward Churchill and Glenn T. Morris, "Key Indian Laws and Cases," in M. Annette Jaimes, ed., *The State of Native America: Genocide, Colonization, and Resistance*, p. 14.

18. Oren Lyons, John Mohawk, et al., *Exiled in the Land of the Free: Democracy, Indian Nations, and the U.S. Constitution*, pp. 324–25.

19. Prucha, *The Great Father*, pp. 808–12.

20. Graham D. Taylor, *The New Deal and American Indian Tribalism: The Administration of the Indian Reorganization Act, 1934–45*, pp. 19–25.

21. Bolt, *American Indian Policy and American Reform*, pp. 116–17.

22. Graham D. Taylor, *The New Deal and American Indian Tribalism*, p. 30.

23. Children born to tribe members who are reservation residents automatically become tribe members if "both parents are of all Indian blood." Children born to tribe members "of all Indian blood" who live off the reservation may be admitted to membership by the Tribal Council. *Constitution and By Laws of the Alabama Coushatta Tribes of Texas*, Article II—Membership, section 1, paragraphs b and c.

24. *Constitution and By Laws of the Alabama-Coushatta Tribes of Texas*, Article III—Governing Body, section 1.

25. James W. Markham, "Alabama-Coushatta Indian Reservation" p. 20.

26. Nash, "The Indians of Texas," p. 25.

27. Ibid., pp. 23–24.

28. Galloway, "Head Teacher or Principal's Term Report, . . . 1931–1932,"

unpublished document, pp. 5, 7. Sam Houston Regional Library and Research Center, Liberty, Texas.

29. Markham, "Alabama-Coushatta Indian Reservation," p. 19.
30. Application for Equalization Aid, 1940–1941, unpublished document. Sam Houston Regional Library and Research Center, Liberty, Texas.
31. Markham, "Alabama-Coushatta Indian Reservation," p. 20.
32. Texas Public School Directory, 1945–1946. Sam Houston Regional Library and Research Center, Liberty, Texas.

This chart demonstrates the growth of the Indian Village School from 1918 to 1945:

Year	Students	Teachers	Grades Taught	Term (Months)
1918–19		1	7	5
1919–20		2	7	6
1920–21		2	7	6
1921–22		2	7	6
1922–23	49	2	7	6
1923–24	55	1	7	6
1924–25	61	1	9	7
1925–26	60	3	9	6
1926–27	58	4	9	7
1927–28	59	3	9	7
1928–29	69	3	9	8
1929–30	59	4	9	8
1930–31	66	4	9	8
1931–32	73	4	9	9
1932–33	75	4	10	9
1933–34	76	4	10	9
1934–35	75	4	10	9
1935–36	76	4	10	9
1936–37	76	4	10	9
1937–38	74	5	9	9
1938–39	73	5	9	9
1939–40	80	5	9	9
1940–41	91	5	9	9
1941–42	94	5	9	9
1942–43	95	5	9	9
1943–44	98	5	9	9
1944–45	103	3	9	9

"The figures in this chart were taken from records in the office of the County Superintendent of Polk County." King, "The Educational Growth of the Alabama and Coushatta Indians of East Texas," p. 33.

33. King, "The Educational Growth of the Alabama and Coushatta Indians of East Texas," p. 34.
34. Andrew Battise, quoted in King, "The Educational Growth of the Alabama and Coushatta Indians of East Texas," p. 35.
35. Jo Ann Battise, personal interview.
36. Alison R. Bernstein, *American Indians and World War II: Toward a New Era in Indian Affairs*, p. 131.
37. Doris A. Paul, *The Navajo Code Talkers*, p. 110.
38. For a more complete account of Ira Hayes's cultural dilemma, see Karal Ann Marling and John Wetenhall, *Iwo Jima: Monuments, Memories, and the American Hero*.
39. Paul, *The Navajo Code Talkers*, pp. 104–106; Walker J. Norcross, "History and Army Service: World Wars I and II," in Keats Begay and Agnes R. Begay, et al., *Navajos and World War II*, pp. 113–14.
40. Bernstein, *American Indians and World War II*, p. 132.
41. Vine Deloria, Jr., and Clifford M. Lytle, *The Nations Within: The Past and Future of American Indian Sovereignty*, p. 190.
42. Daniel Battise, personal interview.
43. Laurine H. Battise, personal interview.
44. Ibid.
45. Lawrine Low Battise and Dedie Williams, personal interviews.
46. Cornell, *The Return of the Native*, pp. 121–23.
47. Donald L. Fixico, *Termination and Relocation: Federal Indian Policy, 1945–1960*, p. 18.
48. Fixico, *Termination and Relocation*, p. 183.
49. Oren Lyons, John Mohawk, et al., *Exiled in the Land of the Free: Democracy, Indian Nations, and the U.S. Constitution*, pp. 288–89.
50. Rebecca L. Robbins, "Self-Determination and Subordination: The Past, Present, and Future of American Indian Governance," in Jaimes, *The State of Native America*, pp. 99–100.
51. Fixico, *Termination and Relocation*, p. 67. See also Patricia K. Ourada, "Dillon Seymour Myer (1950–53)," in Kvasnicka and Viola, eds., *The Commissioner of Indian Affairs*, pp. 293–300.
52. Fixico, *Termination and Relocation*, p. 71.
53. Ibid., pp. 97–98.
54. Ibid., pp. 104–105.
55. National Congress of American Indians, "Important Notice to All Tribes," May 7, 1954. Sam Houston Regional Library and Research Center, Liberty, Texas.
56. Fixico, *Termination and Relocation*, pp. 125–26.
57. Larry O. Cox, Executive Director, Board for Texas State Hospitals and Special Schools, to A. D. Folweiler, Texas Forest Service, October 5, 1951. Sam Houston Regional Library and Research Center, Liberty, Texas.
58. Andrew J. Battise to C. H. Jones, Jr., March 7, 1952. Sam Houston Regional Library and Research Center, Liberty, Texas.

59. Alabama-Coushatta Tribal Meeting minutes, February 13, 1953, p. 1. Sam Houston Regional Library and Research Center, Liberty, Texas.
60. Ibid., p. 2.
61. Addendum to Alabama-Coushatta Tribal Meeting, February 13, 1953, p. 2. Sam Houston Regional Library and Research Center, Liberty, Texas.
62. Ibid., p. 4.
63. Ibid., p. 1.
64. Texas Senate, Senate Concurrent Resolution Number 31, (passed Senate March 26, 1953, passed House April 28, 1953).
65. Alabama-Coushatta Tribal Resolution, June 1, 1953. Sam Houston Regional Library and Research Center, Liberty, Texas.
66. Department of the Interior Information Service, Bureau of Indian Affairs, June 4, 1953.
67. U.S., Congress, House, *A Bill to terminate Federal trust responsibility to the Alabama and Coushatta Tribes of Indians of Texas, and for other purposes.* H.R. 6282, 83 Congress, 1 Sess., 1953, p. 1.
68. U.S., Congress, House, *A Bill to transfer certain lands to the State of Texas to be held in trust for the Alabama and Coushatta Indians, and for other purposes,* H.R. 6547, 83 Congress, 1 Sess., 1953, p. 1.
69. Representative John Dowdy, 7th District of Texas, to Glenn L. Emmons, Commissioner of the Bureau of Indian Affairs, January 16, 1954. Sam Houston Regional Library and Research Center, Liberty, Texas.
70. Ibid.
71. Alabama-Coushatta General Council Resolution, January 18, 1954, "72 For, and 0 Against." Sam Houston Regional Library and Research Center, Liberty, Texas.
72. C. H. Jones, Jr., Alabama-Coushatta Reservation Superintendent, to William Wade Head, January 25, 1954. Sam Houston Regional Library and Research Center, Liberty, Texas.
73. Alabama-Coushatta Tribal Meeting Resolution, January 28, 1954. Sam Houston Regional Library and Research Center, Liberty, Texas.
74. Matthew Bullock, Chairman of the General Council of the Alabama-Coushatta, to the Commissioner of Indian Affairs, through W. Wade Head, January 29, 1954. Sam Houston Regional Library and Research Center, Liberty, Texas.
75. Nash, "The Indians of Texas," p. 21.
76. Wade, *The Alabama Indians of East Texas,* pp. 12–13.
77. The possibility that the trade language was absorbed by the dominant Albamu language was suggested by tribe member Armando Rodriguez. He stated that there are a significant number of Choctaw words in the Alabama language used today, and this was indicative of the Mobilian trade language. Laurine H. Battise remembers her grandfather discussing the "old language" which is no longer spoken.
78. Nash, "The Indians of Texas," p. 20.
79. Ibid., p. 30.

80. Ibid., pp. 22–23.
81. Ibid., p. 27.
82. McClamroch, "History of the Alabama Indian Church," pp. 13–16.
83. Ibid., p. 16.
84. Roland Poncho, personal interview.
85. Nash, "The Indians of Texas," p. 29.
86. Ibid., p. 22.
87. Armando Rodriguez and Joe John, personal interviews.
88. Smither, "The Alabama Indians of Texas," p. 108.
89. Wade, *The Alabama Indians of East Texas*, p. 11.
90. Joe John, personal interview.
91. Zetha Battise, personal interview.
92. Walter Broemer, personal interview.
93. Wade, *The Alabama Indians of East Texas*, p. 16.
94. Jo Ann Battise, personal interview.
95. W. E. S. Folsom-Dickerson, *The White Path* (San Antonio: The Naylor Company, 1965), pp. 26–34.

Chapter 5. Ethnogenesis and Regenesis

1. John Daniel Hammerer, *An Account of a Plan for Civilizing the North American Indians, proposed in the Eighteenth Century.*
2. Donald Charles Fairweather, Jr., *Administrative Planning in Indian Adult Education Based on the Socio-Economic Effects of High School Versus Non-High School Graduation,* pp. 70–71.
3. Walter Broemer, former Alabama-Coushatta Reservation Superintendent, personal interview; "Indian Village Assembly of God to dedicate new church Sunday," *Polk County Enterprise,* April 9, 1981, p. 3c.
4. Walter Broemer, personal interview.
5. Mark Langley, Alabama-Coushatta tribe member and powwow dancer, personal interview.
6. Jack Battise, Alabama-Coushatta tribal elder, personal interview.
7. Zetha Battise and Jack Battise, personal interviews.
8. Deloria, *Custer Died for Your Sins,* p. 196.
9. Bolt, *American Indian Policy and American Reform,* pp. 287–306.
10. Prucha, *The Great Father,* p. 358.
11. Adam Fortunate Eagle, *Alcatraz! Alcatraz!: The Indian Occupation of 1969–1971,* p. 22.
12. Cornell, *The Return of the Native,* pp. 194–97.
13. For an overview of the Red Power movement by a journalist, see Rex Weyler, *Blood of the Land: the Government and Corporate War Against First Nations.*
14. Eagle, *Alcatraz! Alcatraz!,* pp. 46–47.
15. Prucha, *The Great Father,* p. 366.

16. Peter Matthiessen, *In The Spirit Of Crazy Horse*, p. 37.

17. Ibid., pp. 34–36.

18. Ibid., pp. 52–54.

19. Prucha, *The Great Father*, pp. 366–67. Little, however, changed on the Pine Ridge reservation, and many residents resented what they perceived to be an urban Indian organization intruding into their internal affairs. The virtually open warfare continued on the reservation for several years, with widespread terrorism and, according to Wounded Knee participant Michael Haney, over one hundred still unsolved murders taking place.

20. Michael Haney, Creek-Seminole activist, personal interview.

21. Ibid.

22. Jonathan B. Hook, "Powwow Program," First Annual Houston Community College System Powwow and Lou Diamond Phillips Presentation, March 27–28, 1994.

23. Chris Roberts, *Powwow Country*, p. 22–24.

24. Ibid., p. 20.

25. "Indian reservation's tourist push starts in 1962," *Polk County Enterprise*, November 11, 1982, pp. 1–2.

26. Aline Thompson Rothe, *Kalita's People: A History of the Alabama-Coushatta Indians of Texas*.

27. Folsom-Dickerson, *The White Path*, p. 33; Jack Battise, personal interview. Folsom-Dickerson states that Boatman was Coushatta, but Jack Battise remembers that he was Alabama and that his second wife was Coushatta.

28. Folsom-Dickerson, *The White Path*, pp. 26–33.

29. Walter Broemer, personal interview.

30. "First Staff Meeting Under New Superintendent," July 18, 1957, unsigned minutes of meeting.

31. Sylestine, et al., "The Alabama Coushatti Indian Church," first page inside front cover.

32. Walter Broemer, personal interview.

33. "Indian Chief Sylestine Dies," *Polk County Enterprise*, February 27, 1969, p. 1.

34. Debra Battise Kleinman, Alabama-Coushatta tribe member, personal interview.

35. Walter Broemer, personal interview.

36. "Indians Air Gripes At Meeting On Reservation," *Polk County Enterprise*, July 25, 1968, pp. 1, 7; "Request To Fire Indian Superintendent Rejected," *Polk County Enterprise*, October 24, 1968, pp. 1, 6.

37. Walter Broemer, personal interview.

38. Laurine H. Battise, personal interview.

39. "Indian Chiefs Inaugurated In Impressive Ceremony," *Polk County Enterprise*, January 8, 1970, p. 10.

40. "More Than 100,000 Visited Reservation in 1967," *Polk County Enterprise,* February 1, 1968, p. 1.
41. "Okayed For Reservation: Phase 1 Will Include 30-Acre Lake And Supporting Utilities," *Polk County Enterprise,* June 20, 1968, p. 1.
42. "Indians Praised At Dedication," *Polk County Enterprise,* July 19, 1971, pp. 1, 7.
43. "Reservation Boosts Polk Economy," *Polk County Enterprise,* January (page and date unknown) 1968, photocopy.
44. Roland Poncho, Alabama-Coushatta Tribal Council chairman, personal interview.
45. Frances Battise, head nurse and former Tribal Council chairwoman, personal interview.
46. Sylestine, et al., "The Alabama Coushatti Indian Church," first page inside front cover.
47. Stephen Harrigan, "Bury My Heart at the Souvenir Shop," *Texas Monthly* (October, 1975), p. 99.
48. Walter Broemer, Frances Broemer, Jack Battise, personal interviews. Frances recalls that Jack's unwavering commitment to the success of these dances caused their ultimate success. Jack states that some of the dance forms utilized by the Alabama-Coushatta dancers were those taught to them by the Comanches during their 1936 visit.
49. "Indians to Hold Pow-Wow," *Polk County Enterprise,* July 17, 1969, p. 2.
50. Ibid., p. 102.
51. Herman Kelly, "Powwow," *Texas Highways,* (May, 1974), p. 8.
52. Deni Sylestine, Alabama-Coushatta powwow dancer, personal interview.
53. Herman Kelly, "A Red Man in a White Man's World," *Texas Highways* (October, 1971), p. 12.
54. Jack Lowery, "A Celebration of Cultures," *Texas Highways* (November, 1991), p. 49.
55. Stephanie Williams, powwow committee member and Tribal Council member, personal interview.
56. Walter Broemer, personal interview.
57. "Indian Progress Reports Given," *Polk County Enterprise,* December 30, 1971, p. 2.
58. Walter Broemer, personal interview.
59. Lyndon Alec shot two deer. While he was cleaning them in his front yard a young game warden drove by, stopped, and asked to see Alec's hunting license. Alabamas and Coushattas had never purchased licenses to hunt on their land, believing that they had no legal obligation to do so. Alec explained that no one possessed licenses, and that even one of the prominent tribe members, Clayton Sylestine, was cleaning his deer at that very moment. The warden cited Alec, confiscated his deer, and proceeded to Sylestine's home. Clayton was cleaning his deer in the back yard, out of sight from the road. The warden drove in and stated that he had seen

Sylestine as he drove down the road and asked to see his license. This deer was also confiscated.

Justice of the Peace Mary Placker heard the case but was unsure of who had jurisdiction. Walter Broemer contacted the head game warden, Bob Hall, contesting the confiscations and citations. Parks and Wildlife asked Texas Attorney General Jim Maddox for an opinion. The opinion committee ruled in March, 1983, that there was no reservation in Texas. "Maddox's opinion invokes Indians' ire," *Polk County Enterprise,* April 7, 1983, p. 1.; Francis Battise, Clayton Sylestine, Walter Broemer, Frances Broemer, Armando Rodriguez, personal interviews.

60. "Anniversary Celebrated," *Polk County Enterprise,* September 22, 1988, p. 1.

61. The boys spoke first with Mark Bilbo, a mixed-blood Cherokee author of computer manuals, then with the author.

62. Verified Application for Temporary Restraining Order, filed October 13, 1992.

63. Timothy S. Zahniser, "Alabama & Coushatta Tribes v. Big Sandy School District: The Right of Native American Public School Students to Wear Long Hair," *American Indian Law Review* 19 (No. 1, 1994): 228.

64. Danny John, testimony in U.S. 5th Circuit Court, preliminary injunction hearing, January 4, 1993, author's observation.

65. Author's personal observation.

66. Timothy S. Zahniser, "Alabama-Coushatta Tribes v. Big Sandy School District," p. 230.

67. Author's personal observation.

68. Donald Juneau, telephone conversation with Jonathan Hook.

69. Donald Juneau to Jonathan Hook, letter, November 28, 1994.

70. Zetha Battise, personal interview.

71. Jonathan Hook, Introductory sections of the 1995 Grant Proposal submitted to the Presbyterian Self-Development Committee:

> *The purpose of this project is to enhance the self-esteem of our people through increased knowledge and experience of our own unique history and culture. This is critical if we are to survive intact as a people. There are two components to the project: Native American cultural history and Alabama-Coushatta cultural history. The first component will allow five students and five adults to visit other Indian communities and study their history and cultural practices. This will demonstrate that while we are a unique American Indian nation, there are also many similarities among Native Americans throughout the continent. Videos will be taken and subsequently compiled into a comprehensive overview of Native America. This will be an ongoing project with several sites designated for visits each summer. We will camp much of the time and travel in a van or mini-bus.*

The first trip, scheduled for June 1995, will be to the Pine Ridge Lakota Sioux reservation in South Dakota. There we will visit Wounded Knee, the location of the massacre of 300 Sioux women and children (which is frequently perceived to be the pivotal event in Indian history). We will also visit the Little Big Horn battleground in southeast Montana and discuss with the people on the Crow reservation how they remember that event. In subsequent trips we will travel to reservations in the east, to Cherokees in Oklahoma, and we'll retrace the steps of our own migration from Alabama (which was named for us) to Texas.

The second component is the preservation and documentation of our Alabama-Coushatta history and cultural expressions. We will video tape our elders telling stories and singing the old songs in our language. There is no visual record of a community elder making a pine needle or split river cane basket; we will document it. We will discuss with people how their lives on the reservation have changed since they were young, and the direction they would like to see our community take in the future.

A segment will be taped each month and a composite video will be produced each year which will be made available to everyone wishing to know more about our people. It will be utilized to enhance our own knowledge and to combat pervasive racism and misunderstanding through presentations made to the non-Indian community (schools, businesses, churches, etc.). Those youth and community elders directly involved will develop enhanced self-esteem, and the surrounding non-Indian community will be made better aware of the issues facing our people. This record will inform our grandchildren and great-grandchildren about the people who make up their rich heritage. We can turn the tide of despair and hopelessness through exploring and relating our culture and tribal history!

72. Author's personal observation.
73. Zetha Battise and Rochellda Sylestine, personal interviews.

Conclusion

1. Jo Ann Battise, personal interview.
2. Rochellda Sylestine, personal interview.
3. This ceremonial haircut at the age of four months took place on March 2, 1996, at 2:00 P.M.
4. Lucille Silk, Ojibwa tribe member and mental health care professional, personal interview, January, 1996.
5. The author was a chaperone at this conference, and the cited information was obtained through personal observation.
6. A large fire was kindled and maintained by shifts of volunteers during the

conference. While I was sitting at the fire with two of the Alabama-Coushatta young men, they commented about how frustrating it was that no leader would work with them in facing the issue of alcohol and addressing it in a forthright manner.

7. Harrigan, "Bury My Heart at the Souvenir Shop," p. 85.

8. For an analysis of the role of culture broker as mediator, see Margaret Connell Szasz, "Conclusion," in Margaret Connell Szasz, ed., *Between Indian and White Worlds: The Cultural Broker.*

Bibliography

Primary Sources

Unpublished Documents and
Published Primary Documents

Abel, Annie Heloise, ed. *A Report from Natchitoches in 1807 by Dr. John Sibley.*
Indian Notes and Monographs* Number 25. Edited by F. W. Hodge. New
York: Museum of the American Indian, Heye Foundation, 1922.

Adair, James. *The History of the American Indians.* London: Printed for Edward
and Charles Dilly, in the Poultry, 1775.

Alabama-Coushatta General Council Resolution, January 18, 1954. Sam Houston Regional Library and Research Center, Liberty, Texas.

Alabama-Coushatta Presbyterian Church. Session minutes. August 24, 1910.
Murphy Memorial Library. Livingston, Tex.

Alabama-Coushatta Tribal Administration. "First Staff Meeting Under New
Superintendent." Unsigned minutes of meeting. July 18, 1957. Sam Houston Regional Library and Research Center, Liberty, Texas.

Alabama-Coushatta Tribal Meeting minutes. February 13, 1953. Sam Houston
Regional Library and Research Center, Liberty, Texas.

Alabama-Coushatta Tribal Meeting. Addendum to minutes. February 13, 1953.
Sam Houston Regional Library and Research Center, Liberty, Texas.

Alabama-Coushatta Tribal Meeting Resolution. June 1, 1953. Sam Houston Regional Library and Research Center, Liberty, Texas.

Alabama-Coushatta Tribal Meeting Resolution. January 28, 1954. Sam Houston
Regional Library and Research Center, Liberty, Texas.

Alabama-Coushatta Tribes of Texas, *Constitution and By Laws.*

Bartram, William. *The Travels of William Bartram*. Naturalist's ed. Ed. with commentary and annotated index by Francis Harper. New Haven: Yale University Press, 1958.

Battise, Andrew J. Letter to C.H. Jones, Jr. March 7, 1952. Sam Houston Regional Library and Research Center, Liberty, Texas.

Berlandier, Jean Louis. *The Indians of Texas in 1830*. Ed. and intro. by John C. Ewers. Washington, D.C.: Smithsonian Institution Press, 1969.

Black Elk. *Black Elk Speaks: Being the Life Story of a Holy Man of the Oglala Sioux, as told through John G. Neihardt*. 1932. Lincoln: University of Nebraska Press, 1992.

Bolton, Herbert Eugene, ed. and trans. *Athanase De Mezieres and the Louisiana-Texas Frontier: 1768–1780*. 2 vols. Cleveland: The Arthur H. Clark Company, 1914.

Bossu, Jean-Bernard. *Travels in the Interior of North America*. Ed. and trans. by Seymour Feiler. Norman: University of Oklahoma Press, 1962.

Bourne, Edward Gaylord, ed. *Narratives of the Career of Hernando de Soto in the Conquest of Florida, as told by a Knight of Elvas and in a relation by Luys Hernandez de Biedma, Factor of the Expedition, also based on the Diary of Rodrigo Ranjel, his Private Secretary*. 1922. Reprint, New York: AMS Press, 1973.

Bullock, Matthew. Letter to the Commissioner of Indian Affairs, through W. Wade Head. January 29, 1954. Sam Houston Regional Library and Research Center, Liberty, Texas.

Chambers, Mrs. C. W. "Head Teacher or Principal's Term Report based on Teacher's Daily Register to the Superintendent of Public Schools, 1922–1923." Sam Houston Regional Library and Research Center, Liberty, Texas.

Cherokee Nation of Oklahoma. 1994 Cherokee National Holiday Program. Tahlequah, Okla.

Cherokee Nation of Oklahoma. *Constitution*. Article III, Membership. Section One. Ratified June 26, 1976.

Cook, Charles H. "Pima Indians." *Presbyterian Home Missions*. Vol. 11 (August, 1882).

———. Sermon manuscript. October 16, 1898.

Coston, I. A. "Only Indian Reservation in Texas." *Frontier Times*. Vol. 24 (April, 1947).

Coushatta (Louisiana). "Indian Days." *1994 Coushatta Celebration Program*. Kinder, La.

Cox, Larry O. *Letter to A. D Folweiler*. October 5, 1951.

De la Vega, Garcilaso. *The Florida of the Inca*. Ed. and trans. by John Grier Varner and Jeanette Johnson Varner. Austin: University of Texas Press, 1951.

De Vaca, Cabeza. *Adventures in the Unknown Interior of America*. Trans. and annotated by Cyclone Covey, with a new epilogue by William T. Pilkington. Albuquerque: University of New Mexico Press, 1990.

Dowdy, John. Letter to Glenn L. Emmons. January 16, 1954. Sam Houston Regional Library and Research Center, Liberty, Texas.

Du Pratz, M. Le Page. *The History of Louisiana*. Ed. by Joseph G. Tregle, Jr. Published for the Louisiana American Revolution Bicentennial Commission. 1774. Facsimile, Baton Rouge: Louisiana State University Press, 1975.

Fain, Clem, Jr. "East Texas." *Polk County Enterprise,* April, 1928.

Fairweather, Donald Charles Jr. "Administrative Planning in Indian Adult Education Based on the Socio-Economic Effects of High School Versus Non-High School Graduation." Ed.D. dissertation. College of Education, University of Houston, 1977.

Fitzgerald, Herman H. "Application for Equalization Aid, 1940–1941." Principal, Indian Village School. Sam Houston Regional Library and Research Center, Liberty, Texas.

Folsom-Dickerson, W. E. S. *The White Path*. San Antonio: The Naylor Company, 1965.

"Friendly Indians of the Trinity River." Anonymous. (From *Texas Almanac, 1861,* [mistakenly listed as 1860]). *Frontier Times,* Vol. 2 (June, 1925).

Galloway, J. P. "Head Teacher or Principal's Term Report Based on Teacher's Daily Register to the Superintendent of Public Schools, 1931–1932." Sam Houston Regional Library and Research Center, Liberty, Texas.

————. "Head Teacher or Principal's Term Report Based on Teacher's Daily Register to the Superintendent of Public Schools, 1933–1934." Sam Houston Regional Library and Research Center, Liberty, Texas.

Gammel, H. P. N., ed. "An Act Authorizing the President to have Surveyed a Reserve of Land for the Coshattee and Alabama Indians," Approved 25th January, 1840. In *The Laws of Texas, 1822–1897.* 10 vols. Austin: The Gammel Book Company, 1898.

Graham, R. B. Cunninghame. *Hernando de Soto, Together with an Account of One of His Captains, Goncalo Silvestre.* London: William Heinemann, 1912.

Hammerer, John Daniel. *An Account of a Plan for Civilizing the North American Indians, proposed in the Eighteenth Century.* Ed. by Paul Leicester Ford. Brooklyn, New York: Historical Printing Club, 1890.

Harrigan, Stephen. "Bury My Heart at the Souvenir Shop." *Texas Monthly,* October, 1975.

Hart, F. J. "Papagoes." *Presbyterian Home Missionary.* Vol. 14 (February, 1885).

Haynes, Emma R. "The History of Polk County." Essay. 1937. Sam Houston Regional Library and Research Center, Liberty, Texas.

Hook, Jonathan B. Self-Development Grant Proposal. May, 1995. Livingston, Tex. In author's possession.

Indian Village School. Application for Equalization Aid, 1940–1941. Sam Houston Regional Library and Research Center, Liberty, Texas.

"The Indians in Polk County, Texas." (From *Dallas News*). *Frontier Times,* Vol. 5 (October, 1927).

Intertribal Council of Houston. By-Laws. Article II, Membership. Section One. 1978. Houston, Tex. In author's possession.

Jones, C. H. Letter to William Wade Head. January 25, 1954. Sam Houston Regional Library and Research Center, Liberty, Texas.

Juneau, Donald. Letter to Jonathan B. Hook. November 28, 1994. In author's possession.

Kelly, Herman. "A Red Man in a White Man's World." *Texas Highways,* October, 1971.

———. "Powwow." *Texas Highways,* May, 1974.

Kinney, Bruce. *Frontier Missionary Problems: Their Character and Solution.* New York: Fleming H. Revell Company, 1918.

"Lo, the Poor Alabamas." *East Texas Optimist* (Woodville, Tex.). October 30, 1930. From the Beaumont Enterprise, n.d.

Lowery, Jack. "A Celebration of Cultures." *Texas Highways,* November, 1991.

McClamroch, Mrs. R. S. Nettie. "History of the Alabama Indian Church." Essay. Beaumont: 1944.

Merrem, William. "Merrem Tells About His Experiences, An Oral History Interview." *Texas Forestry,* Vol. 24 (September, 1983).

Nash, Roy. "The Indians of Texas." Unpublished Report of the Special Commissioner. March 1931. Sam Houston Regional Library and Research Center, Liberty, Texas.

National Congress of American Indians "Important Notice to All Tribes." May 7, 1954. Sam Houston Regional Library and Research Center, Liberty, Texas.

Northup, Solomon Northup. *Twelve Years A Slave.* Ed. by Sue Eakin and Joseph Logsdon. Baton Rouge: Louisiana State University Press, 1968.

Olmstead, Frederick Law. *A Journey Through Texas: Or, a Saddle-Trip on the Southwestern Frontier.* 1857. Reprint, Austin: University of Texas Press, 1978.

Polk County Enterprise, February, 1968–September, 1988.

"Polk County Historical Sketchbook." Murphy Memorial Library. Livingston, Tex.

Roth, Aline. "Missionaries to Alabama-Coushattas Brought Light to Sun Kee's Dark Cloud." *The Houston Chronicle,* day and month unlisted, 1946.

Schoolcraft, Henry B. *History, Condition and Prospects of the Indian Tribes of the United States: Collected and Prepared Under the Direction of the Bureau of Indian Affairs, Department of the Interior.* Volume V. Facsimile, Philadelphia: J.B. Lippincott and Company, 1855.

Sylestine, Clem, et al. "The Alabama Coushatti Indian Presbyterian Church." Essay prepared by the 1992 Indian Presbyterian Church Historical Committee. Alabama-Coushatta Indian Presbyterian Church Archives

Sylestine, Emily. "Predicament of Alabama Indians Told by Native Girl." *Houston Post-Dispatch.* Quoted in Frontier Times, Vol. 9 (April, 1932).

Taylor, Virginia H. Taylor, ed. *The Letters of Antonio Martinez: Last Spanish Governor of Texas, 1817–1822.* Austin: Texas State Library, 1957.

Texas. Senate. "Special Committee Report." 41 Legislature. Reg. Sess. 1929.

———. Senate Concurrent Resolution number 31. Passed Senate March 26, 1953, passed House April 28, 1953.

Texas Public School Directory, 1945–1946. Austin, Tex. Sam Houston Regional
Library and Research Center, Liberty, Texas.

"Tucson Training School." *Home Missions Monthly*. November, 1893.

U.S. Congress. House. *Report of William Loker and Letters to the Indian Department Relative to the Alabama Indians of Texas*. 62 Cong., 2 Sess., No. 866, July 6, 1912.

———. Report. *Purchase of Land, Livestock, and Agricultural Equipment for Alabama and Coushatta Indians, Texas*. 70 Cong., 1 Sess., No. 824, March 2, 1928.

———. *An act making appropriations to supply deficiencies in certain appropriations for the fiscal year ending June 30, 1928, and prior fiscal years, to provide supplemental appropriations for the fiscal years ending June 30, 1928, and June 30, 1929, and for other purposes*. 70 Cong., 45 Stat. L. 883-900, 1st sess., 1928.

———. *A Bill to terminate Federal trust responsibility to the Alabama and Coushatta Tribes of Indians of Texas, and for other purposes*. H.R. 6282, 83 Congress, 1 Sess., 1953.

———. *A Bill to transfer certain lands to the State of Texas to be held in trust for the Alabama and Coushatta Indians, and for other purposes*. H.R. 6547, 83 Congress, 1 Sess., 1953.

U.S. Congress. Senate. *An act making appropriations for the current and contingent expenses of the Bureau of Indian Affairs, for fulfilling treaty stipulations with various Indian tribes, and for other purposes, for the fiscal year ending June thirtieth, nineteen hundred and nineteen*. 65 Cong., 2 Sess., 40 Stat. L. 586, Sec. 22, 1918.

U.S. Constitution. Art. I, sec. 8, clause 3.

U.S. Fifth Circuit Court. Verified Application for Temporary Restraining Order. Filed October 13, 1992.

Wade, Mary Donaldson. *The Alabama Indians of East Texas*. Livingston, Tex.: Polk County Enterprise, 1936.

Whittmore, Rev. Issac T. "The Pima Indians, their manners and customs," In *Among the Pimas, or, The Mission to the Pima and Maricopa Indians*. Ed. by Mrs. C. W. Martin. Albany, N. Y.: Private Printing for the Ladies' Union Mission School Association, 1893.

Winfrey, Dorman H., ed. *Texas Indian Papers, 1825–1843*. Austin: Texas State Library, 1959.

———. *Texas Indian Papers, 1844–1845*. Austin: Texas State Library, 1960.

———. Winfrey, Dorman H., ed. *Texas Indian Papers, 1846–1859*. Austin: Texas State Library, 1960.

———. *Texas Indian Papers, 1860–1916*. Austin: Texas State Library, 1961.

Winfrey, Dorman H. and Day, James M., eds. *The Indian Papers of Texas and the Southwest, 1825–1916*. Austin: The Pemberton Press, 1966.

Worcester v. Georgia, 31 U.S. (6 Pet.) 515, 8 L.Ed. 483 (U.S. Sup. Ct. 1832).

Interviews

ALABAMA-COUSHATTA TRIBAL MEMBERS

All interviews conducted on the Alabama-Coushatta Reservation, 1994–96.
Daniel Battise
Esther Battise
Eula Battise
Francis Battise
Jack Battise
Jo Ann Battise
Laurine H. Battise
Lawrine Low Battise
Ludie Battise
Melvin Battise
Roland Battise
Zetha Battise
Dorcas Bullock
Danny John
Joe John
Jimmy Johnson
Debra Battise Kleinman
Mark Langley
Delores Poncho (Dine')
Roland Poncho
Yolanda Poncho
Armando Rodriguez
Clayton Sylestine
Deni Sylestine
Mark Sylestine
Rochellda Sylestine
Dedie Williams
Stephanie Williams

OTHER INTERVIEWS

Charles Boudreaux (Cherokee), Houston, 1993
Frances Broemer, Livingston, 1996
Walter Broemer, Livingston, 1996
Michael Haney (Creek/Seminole), Houston, March, 1993
Donald Juneau, Livingston, 1994
Ed Ketcher (Cherokee of Oklahoma), Beaumont, 1996
Lorilee Lipke (Cherokee of Oklahoma), Houston, 1996
Wilma Mankiller (Cherokee of Oklahoma), Houston, 1995
Deborah Scott (Cherokee of Oklahoma), Houston, 1996
Lucille Silk (Ojibwa), White Earth Reservation, Minnesota, January, 1996

Chad Smith (Cherokee of Oklahoma), Tahlequah, Okla., March, 1996
Rose Castillo Vanderslice (Huateca and Zacatecas), Houston, 1995

Secondary Sources

Abernethy, Francis E., ed. *Tales From the Big Thicket.* Austin: University of Texas Press, 1966.

Aitken, Larry P., and Edwin W. Haller. *Two Cultures Meet: Pathways For American Indians to Medicine.* Duluth: University of Minnesota, 1990.

Alba, Richard D. *Ethnic Identity: The Transformation of White America.* New Haven: Yale University Press, 1990.

American Indian Lawyer Training Program, Inc. *Indian Tribes as Sovereign Governments: A Sourcebook On Federal-Tribal History, Law, and Policy.* Oakland, Calif.: American Indian Resources Institute Press, 1988.

Bailey, Garrick, and Roberta Glenn Bailey. *A History of the Navajos: The Reservation Years.* Santa Fe, N. Mex.: School of American Research Press, 1986.

Barker, Rodney, *The Broken Circle: A True Story of Murder and Magic in Indian Country.* New York: Ballantine Books, 1992.

Begay, Keats, and Agnes R. Begay, et al. *Navajos and World War II.* Tsaile, Navajo Nation, Ariz.: Navajo Community College Press, 1977.

Berkhofer, Robert F., Jr. *Salvation and the Savage: An Analysis of Protestant Missions and American Indian Response, 1787–1862.* Westport, Conn.: Greenwood Press, 1977.

———. *The White Man's Indian: Images of the American Indian from Columbus to the Present.* New York: Alfred A. Knopf, 1978.

Bernstein, Alison R. *American Indians and World War II: Toward a New Era in Indian Affairs.* Norman: University of Oklahoma Press, 1991.

Blu, Karen I. *The Lumbee Problem: The making of an American Indian people.* Cambridge: Cambridge University Press, 1980.

Bolt, Christine. *American Indian Policy and American Reform.* London: Allen & Unwin, 1987.

Bowden, Henry Warner. *American Indians and Christian Missions: Studies in Cultural Conflict.* Chicago: University of Chicago Press, 1981.

Brown, Dee. *Bury My Heart at Wounded Knee: An Indian History of the American West.* New York: Henry Holt and Company, 1970.

Bruchac, Joseph. "Notes of a Translator's Son." *Growing Up Native American.* Ed. by Patricia Riley. New York: Avon Books, 1993.

Brumble, H. David III. *American Indian Autobiography.* Berkeley, Calif.: University of California Press, 1990.

Chapman, Malcolm. "Social and Biological Aspects of Ethnicity." In *Social and Biological Aspects of Ethnicity.* Ed. by Malcolm Chapman. New York: Oxford University Press, 1993.

Churchill, Ward. *Fantasies of the Master Race: Literature, Cinema and the Colonization of American Indians.* Ed. by M. Annette Jaimes. Monroe, Maine: Common Courage Press, 1992.

————, and Glenn T. Morris. "Key Indian Laws and Cases." In *The State of Native America: Genocide, Colonization, and Resistance*. Ed. Annette Jaimes. Boston: South End Press, 1992.

Coleman, Michael C. *Presbyterian Missionary Attitudes toward American Indians, 1837–1893*. Jackson: University Press of Mississippi, 1985.

Cook, Minnie A. *Apostle to the Pima Indians: The Story of Charles H. Cook, The First Missionary to the Pimas*. Tiburon, Calif.: Omega Books, 1976.

Cornell, Stephen E. *The Return of the Native: American Indian Political Resurgence*. New York: Oxford University Press, Inc., 1988.

Crow Dog, Mary, and Richard Erdoes. *Lakota Woman*. New York: Harper-Perennial, 1991.

Davis, Richard Beale. *Intellectual Life in the Colonial South, 1585–1763*. 3 vols. Knoxville: University of Tennessee Press, 1978.

DeConde, Alexander. *This Affair of Louisiana*. New York: Charles Scribner's Sons, 1976.

Deloria, Vine Jr., ed. *American Indian Policy in the Twentieth Century*. Norman: University of Oklahoma Press, 1985.

Deloria, Vine Jr. *Custer Died for Your Sins: An Indian Manifesto*. Norman, Oklahoma: University of Oklahoma Press, 1988.

Deloria, Vine Jr., and Clifford M. Lytle. *The Nations Within: The Past and Future of American Indian Sovereignty*. New York: Pantheon Books, 1984.

Densmore, Frances. "The Alabama Indians and Their Music" In *Straight Texas: Publications of the Texas Folk-Lore Society*. Ed. by J. Frank Dobie. Publication Number 13. Austin: Texas Folk-Lore Society, 1937.

De Vos, George, and Lola Romanucci-Ross, eds. *Ethnic Identity: Cultural Continuities and Change*. Chicago: University of Chicago Press, 1982.

Dobyns, Henry F. *Their Number Become Thinned: Native American Population Dynamics in Eastern North America*. Knoxville: University of Tennessee Press, 1983.

Dowd, Gregory Evans. *A Spirited Resistance: The North American Indian Struggle for Unity, 1745–1815*. Baltimore: Johns Hopkins University Press, 1992.

Earle, Duncan M. "Constructions of Refugee Ethnic Identity: Guatemalan Mayas in Mexico and South Florida," In *Reconstructing Lives, Recapturing Meaning: Refugee Identity, Gender, and Culture Change*. Ed. by Linda A. Camino and Ruth M. Krulfeld. Basel, Switzerland: Gordon and Breach Publishers, 1994.

Eriksen, Thomas Hylland, *Ethnicity and Nationalism: Anthropological Perspectives*. Boulder, Colo.: Pluto Press, 1993.

EschBach, Karl. "Shifting Boundaries: Regional Variations in Patterns of Identification as American Indian." Unpublished manuscript in author's possession. 1992.

Everett, Dianna. *The Texas Cherokees: A People Between Two Fires, 1819–1840*. Norman, Oklahoma: University of Oklahoma Press, 1990.

Fitzgerald, Thomas K. *Metaphors of Identity: A Culture-Communication Dialogue*. Albany: State University of New York Press, 1993.

Fixico, Donald L. *Termination and Relocation: Federal Indian Policy, 1945–1960*. Albuquerque: University of New Mexico Press, 1986.

Flores, Dan L., ed. *Jefferson & Southwestern Exploration: The Freeman & Custis Accounts of the Red River Expedition of 1806*. Norman: University of Oklahoma Press, 1984.

Flores, Dan L. "The Red River Branch of the Alabama-Coushatta Indians." *Southern Studies* 16 (Spring, 1977).

Forbes, Jack D. *Black Africans and Native Americans: Color, Race and Caste in the Evolution of Red-Black Peoples*. New York: Basil Blackwell Inc., 1988.

Foreman, Grant. *Sequoyah*. Norman: University of Oklahoma Press, 1959.

Fortunate Eagle, Adam. *Alcatraz! Alcatraz!: The Indian Occupation of 1969–1971*. Berkeley, Calif.: Heyday Books, 1992.

Franco, Jere. "The Alabama-Coushatta and their Texas Friends." *East Texas Historical Journal* 27 (No. 1, 1989).

Frisbie, Charlotte Johnson. *Kinaalda: A Study of the Navajo Girl's Puberty Ceremony*. Salt Lake City: University of Utah Press, 1993.

Gelo, Daniel J., and Tammy J. Morales. "The Alabama-Coushatta Indians: A Research Guide and Bibliography." *Recent Research from The Institute of Texan Cultures Department of Research and Collections* 2 (March, 1992).

Glazer, Nathan, Daniel Patrick Moynihan. *Beyond the Melting Pot*. Cambridge: The Massachusetts Institute of Technology Press and the Harvard University Press, 1963.

Green, Rayna. *Women in American Indian Society*. New York: Chelsea House Publishers, 1992.

Gurr, Ted Robert. *Minorities at Risk: A Global View of Ethnopolitical Conflicts*. Washington, D.C.: United States Institute of Peace Press, 1993.

Hagan, William T. "Quanah Parker." In *American Indian Leaders: Studies in Diversity*. Ed. by R. David Edmunds. Lincoln: University of Nebraska Press, 1980.

Hosmer, James K. *The History of the Louisiana Purchase*. New York: D. Appleton and Company, 1902.

Jacobson, Daniel. "Written Ethnological Report and Statement of Testimony: The Alabama-Coushatta Indians of Texas and the Coushatta Indians of Louisiana." In *Alabama-Coushatta (Creek) Indians*. New York: Garland Publishing, 1974.

Kehoe, Alice Beck. *North American Indians: A Comprehensive Account*. Englewood Cliffs, N. J.: Prentice-Hall, 1981.

Keller, Robert H., Jr. *American Protestantism and United States Indian Policy, 1869–82*. Lincoln: University of Nebraska Press, 1983.

King, Willie Ford. "The Educational Growth of the Alabama and Coushatta Indians of East Texas." Master's thesis. Stephen F. Austin State Teachers College, 1949.

Klios, George. "Our People Could Not Distinguish One Tribe from Another: The 1859 Expulsion of the Reserve Indians from Texas." *Southwestern Historical Quarterly* 98 (Fall, 1994).

Kniffen, Fred B., et al. *The Historic Indian Tribes of Louisiana*. Baton Rouge: Louisiana State University Press, 1987.

Kunitz, Stephen J., and Jerrold E. Levy. *Drinking Careers: A Twenty-five-year Study of Three Navajo Populations*. New Haven: Yale University Press, 1994.

Lame Deer (John Fire), and Richard Erdoes. *Lame Deer: Seeker of Visions*. New York: Simon and Schuster, 1972.

Laslett, Peter. *The World We Have Lost Further Explored: England Before the Industrial Age*. 3rd ed. New York: Charles Scribner's Sons, 1984.

Leach, Douglas Edward. *The Northern Colonial Frontier, 1607–1763*. New York: Holt, Rinehart and Winston, 1966.

Lyons, Oren, and John Mohawk, et al. *Exiled in the Land of the Free: Democracy, Indian Nations, and the U.S. Constitution*. Santa Fe, N. Mex.: Clear Light Publishers, 1992.

Mankiller, Wilma, and Michael Wallis. *Mankiller: A Chief and Her People*. New York: St. Martin's Press, 1993.

Markham, James W. "Alabama-Coushatta Indian Reservation." In *The Handbook of Texas*. Ed. by Walter Prescott Webb. Austin: The Texas State Historical Association, 1952.

Marling, Karal Ann, and John Wetenhall. *Iwo Jima: Monuments, Memories, and the American Hero*. Cambridge: Harvard University Press, 1991.

Martin, Calvin. *Keepers of the Game: Indian-Animal relationships and the Fur Trade*. Berkeley: University of California Press, 1978.

———. "The Metaphysics of Writing Indian-White History." In *The American Indian and the Problem of History*. Ed. by Calvin Martin. New York: Oxford University Press, 1987.

Martin, Howard N. *Myths and Folktales of the Alabama-Coushatta Indians of Texas*. Austin: The Encino Press, 1977.

———. "Polk County Indians: Alabamas, Coushattas, Pakana Muskogees." *East Texas Historical Journal* 17 (No.1, 1979).

Matthiessen, Peter. *In The Spirit Of Crazy Horse*. With an epilogue by Peter Matthiessen and an afterword by Martin Garbus. New York: Penguin Books, 1991.

McLoughlin, William G. *The Cherokees and Christianity, 1794–1870: Essays on Acculturation and Cultural Persistence*. Athens, Ga.: University of Georgia Press, 1994.

Momaday, N. Scott. "Personal Reflections." In *The American Indian and the Problem of History*. Ed. by Calvin Martin. New York: Oxford University Press, 1987.

Nagel, Joane. *American Indian Ethnic Renewal: Red Power and the Resurgence of Identity and Culture*. London: Oxford University Press, forthcoming.

Nash, Gary B. *Red, White and Black: The Peoples of Early America*. Englewood Cliffs, N. J.: Prentice-Hall, Inc., 1974.

Nash, Manning. *The Cauldron of Ethnicity in the Modern World*. Chicago: University of Chicago Press, 1989.

Otis, D.S. *The Dawes Act and the Allotment of Indian Lands*. Norman: University of Oklahoma Press, 1973.

Ourada, Patricia K. "Dillon Seymour Myer (1950–53)." In *The Commissioners of Indian Affairs, 1824–1977*. Ed. by Robert M. Kvasnicka and Herman J. Viola. Lincoln: University of Nebraska Press, 1979.

Paul, Doris A. *The Navajo Code Talkers*. Philadelphia: Dorrance and Company, 1973.

Peebles, Ruth. *There Never Were Such Men Before: The Civil War Soldiers and Veterans of Polk County, Texas, 1861–1865*. Livingston, Tex.: Polk County Historical Commission, n. d.

Prucha, Francis Paul. *American Indian Policy in the Formative Years: The Indian Trade and Intercourse Acts, 1790–1834*. Cambridge: Harvard University Press, 1962.

————. *The Great Father: The United States Government and the American Indians*. 2 Vols. Lincoln: University of Nebraska Press, 1984.

Richardson, Rupert Norval. *Texas: The Lone Star State*. Englewood Cliffs, N. J.: Prentice-Hall, Inc., 1958.

Robbins, Rebecca L. "Self-Determination and Subordination: The Past, Present, and Future of American Indian Governance." In *The State of Native America: Genocide, Colonization, and Resistance*. Ed. by M. Annette Jaimes. Boston: South End Press, 1992.

Roberts, Chris. *Powwow Country*. Helena, Mont.: American and World Geographic Publishing, 1992.

Robinson, W. Stitt. *The Southern Colonial Frontier, 1607–1763*. Albuquerque: University of New Mexico Press, 1979.

Roosens, Eugeen E. *Creating Ethnicity: The Process of Ethnogenesis*. Newbury Park, Calif.: SAGE Publications, Inc., 1989.

Rothe, Aline Thompson. *Kalita's People: A History of the Alabama-Coushatta Indians of Texas*. Waco, Tex.: Texian Press, 1963.

Schmidt, Ronald J. "Language Policy and the Pursuit of Equality: Canada and the United States." In *Ethnic and Racial Minorities in Advanced Industrial Democracies*. Ed. by Anthony M. Messina, Luis R. Fraga, Laurie A. Rhodebeck, and Frederick D. Wright. Contributions in Ethnic Studies Number 29. New York: Greenwood Press, 1992.

Shkilnyk, Anastasia M. *A Poison Stronger Than Love: The Destruction of an Ojibwa Community*. New Haven: Yale University Press, 1985.

Smither, Harriet. "The Alabama Indians of Texas." *Southwestern Historical Quarterly* 36 (Oct., 1932).

Stavenhagen, Rodolfo. *The Ethnic Question: Conflict, Development, and Human Rights*. Shibuya-ku, Tokyo, Japan: United Nations University Press, 1990.

Swanton, John R. *Early History of the Creek Indians*. Bureau of American Ethnology Bulletin 73. Washington, D.C.: Smithsonian Institution, 1922.

————. *Myths of the Southeastern Indians*. Bureau of American Ethnology. Bulletin 88. Washington, D.C.: Smithsonian Institution, 1929.

————. "Social Organization and Social Usages of the Indians of the Creek Confederacy." *Forty-Second Annual Report of the Bureau of American Ethnology, 1924–1925*. Washington, D.C.: Government Printing Office, 1928.

Szasz, Margaret Connell. "Conclusion." In *Between Indian and White Worlds: The Cultural Broker.* Ed. by Margaret Connell Szasz. Norman: University of Oklahoma Press, 1994.

Taylor, Graham D. *The New Deal and American Indian Tribalism: The Administration of the Indian Reorganization Act, 1934–45.* Lincoln: University of Nebraska Press, 1980.

Thompson, Richard H. *Theories of Ethnicity: A Critical Appraisal.* Contributions in Sociology Number 82. New York: Greenwood Press, 1989.

Thornton, Russell. *American Indian Holocaust and Survival: A Population History Since 1492.* Norman: University of Oklahoma Press, 1987.

Trelease, Allen W. *Indian Affairs in Colonial New York: The Seventeenth Century.* Ithaca, N. Y.: Cornell University Press, 1960.

Trennert, Robert A., Jr. *Alternative to Extinction: Federal Indian Policy and the Beginnings of the Reservation System, 1846–51.* Philadelphia: Temple University Press, 1975.

———. "William Medill (1845–49)." In *The Commissioners of Indian Affairs, 1824–1977.* Ed. by Robert M. Kvasnicka and Herman J. Viola. Lincoln: University of Nebraska Press, 1979.

Unrau, William E. "Lewis Vital Bogy (1866–67)." In *The Commissioners of Indian Affairs, 1824–1977.* Ed. by Robert M. Kvasnicka and Herman J. Viola. Lincoln: University of Nebraska Press, 1979.

Van den Berghe, Pierre L. *The Ethnic Phenomenon.* New York: Elsevier North Holland, Inc., 1981.

Vaughn, Alden T. *New England Frontier: Puritans and Indians, 1620–1675.* Rev. ed. New York: W.W. Norton and Company, 1979.

Vecsey, Christopher. *Imagine Ourselves Richly: Mythic Narratives of North American Indians.* New York: HarperCollins, 1991.

Walker, Williston. *A History of the Christian Church.* 3rd rev. ed. New York: Charles Scribner's Sons, 1918. Third revised edition by Robert T. Handy, 1970.

Weyler, Rex. *Blood of the Land: the Government and Corporate War Against First Nations.* Philadelphia: New Society Publishers, 1992.

Wilson, Terry P. "Blood Quantum: Native American Mixed Bloods." In *Racially Mixed People in America.* Ed. by Maria P. P. Root. Newbury Park, Calif.: SAGE Publications, 1992.

Wood, Peter H., Gregory A. Waselkov, and M. Thomas Hatley, eds. *Powhatan's Mantle: Indians in the Colonial Southeast.* Lincoln: University of Nebraska Press, 1989.

Yinger, John Milton. *Ethnicity: Source of Strength? Source of Conflict?* Albany: State University of New York Press, 1994.

Zahniser, Timothy S. *"Alabama & Coushatta Tribes v. Big Sandy School District*: The Right of Native American Public School Students to Wear Long Hair." *American Indian Law Review* 19 (No. 1, 1994).

Index

Siache, 30
Sibley, Dr. John, 29–30
Silk, Lucille, 105
Smith, Chad, 6
Smith, Rev. William Albert, 60
Smither, Harriet, 79
Snider, Andy. *See photo gallery*
sofkee, 54
Soweto, IX
Stephen F. Austin State University, 69
stickball (*tele, kopochee*), 23, 33, 52–53,
    79, 102
stomp dance, 13, 50
Sunkee Mikko. *See* Charles Thompson
supratribalism, 11
Swan, Maj. Caleb, 23
swept yards, 56
Sylestine, Chief Bronson Cooper, 52,
    57, 66, 89–90. *See also photo gallery*
Sylestine, Clemson, 75
Sylestine, Cora, 67, 90–91
Sylestine, Deni, XVI, 92
Sylestine, Emily, 49
Sylestine, Joseph K., 45
Sylestine, Lizzie, 54
Sylestine, Mark, XVI, 69
Sylestine, Rochellda, XVI, 97, 108
Sylestine, Chief William Clayton, XII,
    XVI. *See also photo gallery*

Taylor, Rev. Nathaniel, 39
television, 50, 60
Tenney, Rev. S. F., 45–46, 48
termination policy, 70–77
Texas Indian Bureau, 34
Texas Board of Control, 65
Texas Commission on Indian Affairs,
    93
Texas revolution, 31
theological transformation, 46–49
Thomason, Lillian, 66
Thompson, Chief Charles Martin
    (Sunkee), 40, 57. *See also photo gallery*
Thompson, Richard, 14
Thompson, Sub-chief, 38

Thornton, Russell, 20
Throckmorton, Gov. James W., 39
time concept, 18–19
Tombigbee River, 22
tourism, 88–93
town sites, 33
town layout, 23
traditional medicine, 47
Trail of Broken Treaties, 85–86
transportation, 55
Tribal Council, 65
Truman, President Harry, 70–71
Tucson Indian School, 50–51

United Native Indian Tribal Youth
    (UNITY), 105
utensils, 55

Wade, Mary Donaldson, 79–80
Washington Delegation (1928), 40–41
westward migration, 28
White, Rev. Thomas Ward, 45
White Earth, 105
white health care, 51
white response to missionaries, 45–46
Whitside, Capt. Samuel, 39
Whittmore, Rev. Issac, 42
Williams, Bryan, 93
Williams, Dedie, XV, 44, 49, 53, 69
Williams, Douglas Jr. *See photo gallery*
Williams, Emanuel, 94–96
Wilson, Terry B., 7
witches, 49
World War One, 40
World War Two, 67–69
Wounded Knee, 108
Wounded Knee standoff, 85–87
Wovoka, 42

Yazoo River, 22
yukchee, 54

Zimmerman, Commissioner William,
    70
Zimmerman Plan, 70–71